Every Prayer Answered:

Hidden Secrets of the Art of Prayer

Michael Shank

Beloved, I wish above all things that thou mayest prosper and be in health, even as thy soul prospereth.

–John, 3 John 2:2

Therefore, I say unto you, what things soever ye desire, when ye pray, believe that ye receive them, and ye shall have them.

–Jesus, Mark 11:24

Ask, and ye shall receive, that your joy may be full.

–Jesus, John 16:24

READER REVIEW

Brother Mike does it again! Another masterful work as he puts "muscle" into his research, study, and life application on a journey of in-depth prayer and the mystery of "Christ in us" – within Me a Baptized Believer!

He walks us through the scriptures with the keys to the doors of prayer, challenging the Believer to test & prove God's Word truly moves mountains. Are there hidden doors/secrets of prayer to unlock that the Believer has yet to open?

YES! As Mike (and Jonetta) take us on their journey into the closet of prayer, as well as real life stories of people, the excitement of the scriptures through the lens of prayer unfolds through the lives of Bible characters and the exercise of prayer.

You will experience a level of knowledge and understanding about "assumptive belief" that many have yet to embody, for me personally it's because of a lack of teaching/study and I haven't applied the power of my spiritual mind and feelings displaying "Christ in me" – until NOW!

Not only will the Believer find this book life changing to unlocking the scriptures hidden gems of how to pray for our desires, the abundant life, &

cultivating the "garden of our mind," but for the lost soul seeking Christ in you, the hope of glory.

Mike uncovers that the plan of salvation and the plan of prayer intertwine beautifully. Jesus is asking, "What do you want of Me?" But have we learned how to pray in order to respond to His question? Mike helps the reader answer this question using the proper tools of application with practice, discipline, and testing/proving the mystery of Christ in me – the art of prayer is the key to unlocking the Door.

I shall test Him and see that the "End is my Beginning!" Christ is within Me!

Jill Jones
Greenfield, IN

READER REVIEW

I found this book very useful and enlightening. I have practiced several of the concepts in this book throughout my Christian life with marvelous results.

I never thought much however about visualization of the end result of my prayer but always believed that God could do exceedingly, abundantly above all that we ask or think according to the power that worketh in us. Eph. 3:20.

The story and information made me feel happy, excited and sometimes it stopped me in my tracks to retrace and examine what I had read. It challenged me to explore more about prayer and to study more in general in order to put the scriptures deep into the garden of my mind.

I believe that the information taken from this book will be life changing when practiced. Remember to keep an open mind, an open Bible and a highlighter.

Hang on for the ride of your life because this is no ordinary book.

–Gena Jeffery
Bethesda, AR

1

Your Power Within

*Pray for my soul. More things are wrought by prayer
than this world dreams of: Wherefore, let thy voice,
rise like a fountain for me night and day.*

— Alfred Tennyson
Idylls of the King

IF you are one that moves mountains with your prayers, then you already know the secrets to the art of true prayer. For the rest of us…

An elderly woman stood at her bedroom window staring at the mountain beyond and contemplated Jesus' words in Mark 11:23: "*For verily I say unto you, That whosoever shall say unto this mountain, Be thou removed, and be thou cast into the sea; and shall not doubt in his heart, but shall believe that those things which he saith shall come to pass; he shall have whatsoever he saith.*"

"Be thou removed, and be thou cast into the sea!" she exclaimed at the mountain. Then she climbed into her bed and fell fast asleep.

The following morning, she leapt from her bed and rushed to the window– the mountain was still there.

"Oh," she murmured, "I knew it wouldn't work." We long for the faith that moves mountains.

We crave the knowledge that would give to us such freedom and liberty– a power within us to move any mountain on our path.

Let me tell you that you can experience that power. It comes through a discovery of small bits of information previously withheld and unknown; additionally, it requires another examination of the scriptures. Finally, you will experience this mountain-moving power through a specific technique in prayer.

The knowledge I share in the pages to follow is nothing at all new– it's ancient, but not commonly known. It's a knowledge that's taken me some thirty plus years to discover, and it's taken several more years of personal study, application, and experimentation.

Paul wrote, "*Now unto him that is able to do exceeding abundantly above all that we ask or think, according to the power that worketh in us* (Ephesians 3:20)." What is this power that works in us? He, this great power within, is able to somehow do much more than we ask or think? Yes. He is able and very willing.

He who is referred to as this power within is Jesus Christ, and He makes one simple demand of all of us… to believe. What I've discovered is that we *must* believe with all of our hearts, but the specific method of executing our belief in a way that moves mountains has been undiscovered and undefined. When a critical piece of information is unknown, the puzzle is incomplete, and we can't see the entire picture. Our ability to apply our faith in Jesus Christ toward moving the greatest obstacles in our lives is then incomplete. This results in ineffectiveness– failure in prayer.

Failure in prayer leads to deep discouragement. Discouragement is a seed that, once planted in the garden of the mind, may grow into a destruction of faith.

I am, in this story, going to share with you information gathered through extensive study combined with years of consistent experimentation through trial and error. The results are nothing short of remarkable.

The goal of this book is to provide you with this information in the most complete form so that you may test it for yourself and experience this greatest of all mysteries among the Gentiles– *Christ in you*, the hope of glory (Col. 1:27).

I tell you that this power– His power, is within you, but you've not known how to realize it.

2
God's Will

This book is for the Christian. The Christian is, according to the Bible, one who has obeyed the gospel of Jesus Christ (Acts 2:38-47).

A proper and full understanding of the elements, methods, and expectations of prayer is a foundational principle on which Christians exist. The path of prayer is paramount in applying and living out the teachings of Jesus toward a transformative life experience.

The ideas and concepts regarding prayer as taught by Jesus Christ reveal that the key to all success is in His teaching that "we already have what we ask Him for" (Mark 11:24). He said, *"Therefore I say unto you, What things soever ye desire, when ye pray, believe that ye receive them, and ye shall have them (Ibid)."*

Believe that ye *receive them*, and ye *shall have them.* To believe that you *have received something* that you don't currently have (*in order to receive it*) is a bizarre concept. It's a teaching that may, on the outset, seem foolish– a great stretch of the imagination.

To act on His teaching and to apply it within the heart and mind requires the use of the imaginative faculty, because current reality surrounds you and assaults your senses with the its accusation, "You do *not* have what you've asked for!"

So, here is the Lord's premise: Bring your desire to Him in prayer, and believe that you have received it. Do this and you will receive it.

His premise is absolute and without negotiation, as it is clearly set forth in the scriptures. The current problem is that most do not and will not believe Him regarding His instructions for proper and successful prayer. Those who will accept His words do not know *how* to employ such strange instructions.

Additionally, for those who have the courage to act on His words in faith don't know how to remain faithful to the idea that they've received what they don't see.

You and I must be completely convinced that we already have what we've asked for (past tense) so that we may receive (future tense) what we asked for. However, we see that those convinced of receiving were the ones who received.

You might, at first glance, infer that this may be in opposition to God's will; however, that is not the case. Jesus emphasized praying in alignment with God's will. In the Garden of Gethsemane, Jesus prayed, "*Yet not as I will, but as you will*" (Matt. 26:39). This attitude reflects an ultimate submission to God's plan– the central theme in *the way.*

Jesus provided the model for prayer in what is commonly known as The Lord's Prayer (Matt. 6:9-13). This prayer encompasses worship, submission to God's will, daily dependence on God, forgiveness, and deliverance from evil. It serves as a template for believers, encapsulating the essential elements of a life aligned with the Way.

Faith and persistence are foundation stones of prayer, as Jesus taught that prayer should be accompanied by faith and persistence. Again, He stated, "*Therefore I tell you, whatever you ask for in prayer, **believe that you have received it**, and it **will be yours*** (Mark 11:24)." This text reveals His teaching that prayer requires an unusual measure of belief, or faith; persistence– the second component required, is seen in the parable of the persistent widow (Luke 18:1-8), as it reveals the believer's need to pray continually, and to not lose heart.

The way as described in the New Testament is intricately connected to the life of prayer, as taught and exemplified by Jesus Christ. Prayer is not just a ritual, but a foundational practice that sustains baptized believers on their spiritual journey.

By adhering to Jesus' instructions on prayer–practicing sincerity, seeking private communion with God through true prayer, maintaining faith and persistence, and aligning with God's will, Christians walk in *the way* that leads unto life.

What you and I desire is two-fold: we want to escape Hell and damnation to live in eternity with God, our Father, and we want guidance and blessings in the here and now.

This book will reveal to you the secrets to the hidden art of prayer. It will reveal truth regarding how to truly pray. You are about to discover the practical methods required so that you can and will receive your answer to every prayer.

We want to avoid the things which impede and neutralize our prayers, such as "asking amiss", asking with improper motives, and asking selfishly for our own lusts. Most are not able to define what it is to ask "amiss", therefore, they often mis-categorize their poor prayer results under this label.

This book is intended to reveal to the Christian the hidden techniques of the art of successful prayerful.

The successful prayer is a prayer that brings results. This is what men crave. Men desire to find the cause in the law of "cause and effect".

This book will reveal pieces of text from the first century that were suppressed for reasons unknown, as the missing information aligns, as you will see, with the remote text of the scriptures and Christ's teachings on prayers.

Why this book on prayer?

The inspiration for this work originated in the author's personal failures with prayer, and his observations of other's failures and frustrations– observations spanning across thirty years. Thousands of believers pray with great sincerity under urgent need and desire, and in the name of Jesus, and see no results. Great despair and discouragement caused by unanswered prayer leads man toward a departure of the faith.

Further inspiration for this work was increased after and upon a deep study of the true methods of prayer that was "peaked" upon the findings of textual information from the first century which has been suppressed throughout the ages.

The author has, after implementing the information disclosed in this work, experienced answers to his prayers that are nothing short of "miraculous".

The author's previous works have, through the grace and blessings of God, given him a large audience of Christians. His interactions with them have revealed that a vast majority of these men and women in Christ suffer with, and are deeply discouraged by, unanswered prayer.

He's seen the devastating effects of this condition throughout the church and across the country, with such effects leading to a decline in membership and activity, and a literal contraction– a shrinking of the body of Christ.

I, the author, have resisted in writing and sharing this information and my personal experiences of miraculous success in prayer for two primary reasons: this information may be misunderstood, and it may be perceived as a "new" teaching.

With this risk in mind, I have taken great efforts to cite every scriptural evidence that established and proves every idea and concept herein, thus building this work upon the foundation of our plea that we give a "thus saith the Lord" for our every belief.

Prayer, as it relates to our desires, requires honest discussions. What do we want when we contemplate our spiritual position in Christ? Does our desire align with His will? Can I, an average man in Christ, realistically expect to receive the more abundant life that He promised?

I hold no lofty position, nor do I hold a Masters in Theology, nor Doctorate of Divinity. I am an average man. I desire what you desire. I want such things as:

- Eternal salvation
- A closer relationship with the Father and His Son
- Forgiveness when I make a mistake and fall short in behavior or example
- A loving and supportive family
- Quality friendships
- Good health
- An income that provides for my family's need, with some left over for the future

- A work that is meaningful and offers a reasonable level of respect and stability
- An opportunity to provide good gifts to my children and grandchildren
- Opportunities to give to others, and to help those in need
- A future that is bright and hopeful
- An opportunity to make a real and positive difference in someone's life
- And a faith that is active, and alive, and practical, with fruits that can be experienced

Are these points of desire in accord with God's will for our lives? Of course they are.

I assert that these desires are certainly in alignment with God's will, for God so loved us that He gave His only begotten Son who would come to die on a cross as our substitute – the propitiation for our sins, not His, for He had no sin.

God's wants good things for you, just as you want good things for your children and grandchildren. How can we know this? God told us through inspiration via John in 3 John 2:2, *"Beloved, I wish above all things that thou mayest prosper and be in health, even as thy soul prospereth."*

The Lord said, through John, that His *wish above all things* is that that we prosper and be in good health. This is His wish above all other things.

Do you believe that this is God's wish for you? Unfortunately, I have found that the vast majority of Christians believe a wish for prosperity and good health (God's wish for us above all things) is a wish that is "amiss".

Do you pray for bad health, or to be impoverished, or to spend your life in a *hell on earth*? Of course you don't. We– all of us, wish for a more abundant life, and a life of good health, and an eternal home in Paradise. This is the wish of the Lord for us, and it is, according to Him, His wish above all other things.

When a well-intentioned Christian discourages you from entertaining your wish to prosper and to be in good health as the Lord wants for you, be cautious, as their perception of God's will may have been formed from their past failures and ignorance of the scriptures.

I do not promote a "prosperity gospel," or a "name it and claim it philosophy". I advocate what the

Bible advocates. Jesus came to bring us life, and life more abundantly (Jo. 10:10) upon the virtues of love, goodness, right-thinking, and service to others.

"For I know the thoughts that I think toward you, saith the Lord, thoughts of peace, and not of evil, to give you an expected end (Jer. 29:11)." God thinks thoughts of peace toward us, and to give us an expected end.

I'm going to share with you in the pages of this book specific scriptural concepts that have been unidentified, unknown, and not taught. These biblical concepts and the execution of the ideas will give you the necessary tools to receive your every prayer answered.

I give to you the secrets of the hidden art of prayer.

<u>3</u>
Your Desire

Unanswered prayer will, in many cases, become the greatest point of discouragement to mankind in his search for God. This fact cannot be overstated.

When a sincere soul approaches the throne of God in prayer, he is in need. He is in search of the Father.

How many of us who, when confronted with our child's need, will turn him away empty-handed? How many times have you heard another say:

"I prayed, and God didn't answer."

"God was absent in my time of troubles."

"I prayed till I was blue in the face, and God never answered."

"I pray and pray and pray, and nothing happens."

"Praying doesn't seem to make much difference in my life."

"God left me, so I left Him."

"Your thoughts and prayers mean nothing."

"Pray to your 'sky-daddy' – he ain't there – he never answers."

Why can't man know without a shadow of doubt that when he turns to God in prayer, he will receive the answers he is seeking?

May I tell you that he can.

Mankind can, without doubt, pray and receive an answer to his prayer– his every prayer can be answered. Every prayer answered is the objective to all prayer; it can be experienced in the life of every Christian.

While this assertion is bold, it is completely true. This assertion made to you, and all who read this book, will be proven within the pages that follow. More importantly, you'll prove it in your own life.

If you will commit to putting into practice these things I share with you herein, you will live and experience the life that Jesus promised to all who follow Him:

> *"The thief cometh not, but for to steal, and to kill, and to destroy: I am come that they might have life, **and that they might have it more abundantly** (John 10:10)."*

Our Lord cannot lie, as the Hebrew writer said, *"it was impossible for God to lie (Hebrews 6:18)"*. His promise of an abundant life must, therefore, be true. It must be true to all who are in Christ.

Prayer and the answer thereof are built upon the foundation of Christ's statement recorded in Mark 11:24:

> *"Therefore, I say unto you, what things soever ye desire, when ye pray, believe that ye receive them, and ye shall have them."*

It may be said that it is pursuant to this premise that all of Christ's works were executed and verified.

Furthermore, I assert that the elements found in Christ's instructions on prayer as found in Mark 11:24 are not only found in practice as portrayed in the numerous stories in the Bible, but His instructions also contain the hidden elements for which all men can achieve and realize their every prayer answered.

You'll see it in the following story found in the previous chapter of Mark where Jesus confronted a blind man. And, as you'll see, Jesus employs this teaching in practicality to perform what all deem as a miracle. Mark 10:46-52 states:

> *"And they came to Jericho: and as he went out of Jericho with his disciples and a great*

number of people, blind Bartimaeus, the son of Timaeus, sat by the highway side begging. And when he heard that it was Jesus of Nazareth, he began to cry out, and say, Jesus, thou son of David, have mercy on me. And many charged him that he should hold his peace: but he cried the more a great deal, Thou son of David, have mercy on me. And Jesus stood still, and commanded him to be called. And they call the blind man, saying unto him, Be of good comfort, rise; he calleth thee. And he, casting away his garment, rose, and came to Jesus. And Jesus answered and said unto him, What wilt thou that I should do unto thee? The blind man said unto him, Lord, that I might receive my sight. And Jesus said unto him, Go thy way; thy faith hath made thee whole. And immediately he received his sight, and followed Jesus in the way."

Jesus confronts a blind man named Bartimaeus on the side of the highway. He asks, "*What wilt thou that I should do unto thee?*" This is the question that Jesus asks of all men:

"What do you want of Me?"

Herein lies the reason for Christ's instruction in Mark 11:24, *"Therefore, I say unto you, what things soever ye desire"*.

Jesus asked Bartimaeus what he desired. Bartimaeus, like all of us, desired salvation. What was salvation, at that moment, to Bartimaeus? Salvation to Bartimaeus was sight.

Bartimaeus replied, *"Lord, that I might receive my sight."*

Consider that salvation to the poor is money. Salvation to the weak is strength. Salvation to the sick is health. Salvation to the imprisoned is freedom. Salvation to the lame is mobility. Salvation to the dumb is intellect. Salvation to the constricted is expansion. Salvation to the deaf is hearing. Salvation to the homeless is a home. Salvation to the broken is restoration.

What is "salvation" to **you** at this moment? Dear reader, what is it that **you now desire**? What is "salvation" (your current and most urgent need) in the here and now?

Jesus responded to Bartimaeus with a shocking and somewhat bizarre command, *"Go thy way; thy faith hath made thee whole (Mark 10:52)."*

The shock in His statement is clear – He didn't say, "I now give thee thy sight, you are healed." Jesus, instead, responded in a very strange way, as His response implies the thought, *"Go on– it's done!"*

Jesus was applying His words that we find later in Mark 11:24, *"Believe that ye receive (and you will receive)."*

Dear reader, this is not new– we've just missed it.

The Scripture says, *"and immediately he* [Bartimaeus] *received his sight, and followed Jesus in the way"*.

Most have completely missed this practical, eternal, and ever-present meaning of this event, and how this story discloses the secret of prayer.

Bartimaeus was told by Jesus, *"go thy way"* because Bartimaeus' faith had *"made him whole"*.

Herein lies a great secret. *"When ye pray, believe that ye receive them, and ye shall have them"*.

What is the secret? When *you* pray, *believe* that *you already have what you desire.* Believe that your wish is what God wishes for you. *Believe that your wish is fulfilled already*; for it is through obedience to the command to *believe that ye receive* (believe at this moment that you have received what you desire– "assumptive belief"), and you will receive it. It is a spiritual law that some call the Law of Assumption. The law originates in Christ's words:

> *Ask and **it will be given to you**; seek and you will find; knock and the door will be opened to you.* Matthew 7:7

> *Jesus answered and said unto them, Verily I say unto you, If ye have faith, **and doubt not**, ye shall not only do this which is done to the fig tree, but also if ye shall say unto this mountain, Be thou removed, and be thou cast into the sea; **it shall be done**.* Matthew 21:21

> *Therefore I say unto you, What things soever ye desire, when ye pray, **believe that ye receive them, and ye shall have them**.* Mark 11:24

> *And I say unto you, Ask, and **it shall be given you**; seek, and ye shall find; knock, and it shall be opened unto you.* Luke 11:9

*And whatsoever ye shall **ask in my name, that will I do,** that the Father may be glorified in the Son. If ye shall ask any thing in my name, I will do it.* John 14:13-14

*And this is the confidence that we have in him, that, if we ask any thing according to his will, he heareth us: And if we know that he hear us, **whatsoever we ask, we know that we have the petitions that we desired** of him.* 1 John 5:14-15

Jesus is teaching you that your prayer and the resultant answer is completely contingent upon your ability to believe that you have already received your desire. This is a hidden secret in the art of prayer.

It is through the application of this command of Jesus Christ, and our obedience to that command– the instruction to believe that your wish is already fulfilled, or to believe that you receive them, that you receive your wish.

Jesus instructed mankind regarding the secret to eternal salvation in His command, *"He that believeth and is baptized shall be saved* (Mark 16:16)." Jesus, in like manner, instructs mankind regarding the secret to answered prayer in His command, *"He that desires and believes he has received will receive* (Mark 11:24, paraphrased)."

Eternal salvation (the salvation of our eternal soul) is completely contingent upon our obedience of two elements within Christ's command in Mark 16:16: 1) belief, and 2) baptism. Application and obedience results in the saving of our souls.

Answer to prayer (temporal and immediate salvation via reception of our immediate needs through prayer) is completely contingent upon our obedience of two elements within Christ's command in Mark 11:24: 1) prayer, and 2) belief that we have received. Application and obedience results in our receiving the answer, which is a type of "immediate salvation" from our urgent and immediate needs.

This is one piece– a secret to the hidden art of prayer.

Bartimaeus wanted salvation (sight), and prayed to the Lord for his sight. The Lord replied to Bartimaeus to go his way because he had his sight!

How? If Bartimaeus could believe that he received his desire, he would have it. His assumptive belief (faith) made him whole (was the conduit whereby he received his sight– his salvation).

We find that Christ's teaching is a solid and unchangeable spiritual principle:

"Therefore, I say unto you, what things soever ye desire, when ye pray, believe that ye receive them, and ye shall have them."

Jesus' reply reveals His teaching of a spiritual law that we refer to as *assumptive belief.* Assumptive belief is, at its core, the creative power within man. Assumptive belief compels the question and behaviors:

- What do you desire?
- Confront Jesus Christ in prayer.
- Assume that you have your desire.

If you can believe in Christ's words, and accept His instructions as an immutable principle– a law, you will enter into prayer with a radical change of mind (repentance). This is the true art of prayer.

John reiterated Christ's teaching in his first letter to Christians located in modern-day Turkey:

"And if we know that he hear us, whatsoever we ask, we know that we have the petitions that we desired of him." 1 John 5:15

This is the law of assumptive belief. I assume that I have my petitions desired of him; therefore, I receive my desires per His law.

The reasons why we don't receive answers to our prayers are numerous, but the primary reason is because that we have never been taught about Christ's spiritual law of assumptive belief; therefore, we've never been taught how to pray properly.

Why? The answer is because most of our teachers were never taught how to pray properly. We've read it a thousand times and missed it each time. It's not new– we've just missed it.

Paul wrote, *"Now unto Him that is able to do exceeding abundantly above all that we ask or think, according to the power that worketh in us* (Eph. 3:20). Above all that [much more than] we ask [pray] or think [imagine in our heart], according to the power that worketh [the power is the Father, Son, and Holy Spirit] in us [within us]. The power of the Great I AM (Exo. 3:14), His Son, and the Spirit working from within us is enabled through the power of *our assumptive belief* for which we hold.

Assumptive belief is a practical discipline inferred from Christ's statement, *"what things soever ye desire, when ye pray,* **believe that ye receive them, and ye shall have them**".

Christians are, generally speaking, ignorant of that which Jesus spoke of that He called *"the way"*. In Mark 10:52, at the end of Jesus' confrontation with Bartimaeus, it is written, *"and followed Jesus in* **the way** (latter part of verse)." Remember that Jesus said in the beginning of His response to Bartimaeus, *"Go thy way"* (Mark 10:52).

This simple and obscure command of Christ to *"go thy way"* is Christ's revelation to the hearer that his prayers are answered; our response to His answer upon our recognition of our answered prayer [to believe that we have received what we asked for in prayer] is to then follow Jesus *in His way, believing without doubt that we have received* **(before we see the answer made manifest).** This is what brings the answer into reality.

Jesus is *the way,* and *assumptive belief* is the power within all prayer. Assumptive belief is one of the most challenging disciplines that one can embolden themselves to believe in and commit to, and it is the only way to realize your answer.

I will show you in the following pages how to learn this art, and how to employ this discipline into your daily life and routine; and you will, like Bartimaeus, receive your sight.

<u>4</u>

Go Thy Way

And Jesus said unto him, Go thy way; thy faith hath made thee whole. And immediately he received his sight, and followed Jesus in the way.

–Jesus Christ

Gospel of Mark [10:52; KJV]

It is taught throughout all of "Christendom" that Jesus Christ was the Son of God, and a historical figure who existed two-thousand years ago.

While this teaching is certainly factual, for us to teach or perceive the Bible as "mere history" is to do disservice to the soul, and it is to rob the soul of the Bible's applications for today. The Bible is more than a historical document. It is "food" for the soul.

When we fail to find and understand the deep phycological meanings hidden within allegorical narratives, we relegate the Bible to a mere "historical document" that is meaningless and ineffective in providing us with practical, relevant, real-life knowledge in the here and now.

You see, Jesus is alive in the here and now (Revelation 1:18), and He rules at the right hand of the Father (Acts 7:55-56), and He constantly intercedes on our behalf to the Father (Romans 8:34).

Jesus reigns in His kingdom in the here and now, but His kingdom is not of this world (John 18:36) – *it is in you* (Luke 17:21). It is a "spiritual" kingdom, and you are a spirit in whom the kingdom exists.

The kingdom of God is within you (Jo. 17:21).

God is in you (John 14:20; 1 John 4:16).

God's Spirit dwells in you (Romans 8:9).

You yourself are the temple of God (1 Cor. 3:16), as God does not dwell in temples made by human hands (Acts 7:48).

God dwells not in sanctuaries or churches or synagogues or the like (Acts 17:24), as you are the temple made without hands.

You are that temple, and the kingdom of God is within you (Luke 17:21).

Do you not know yourselves, that Jesus Christ is in you (2 Cor. 13:5)?

You and I are Bartimaeus– we have needs. Jesus Christ who is alive within us, and He continually asks, "*What do you want Me to do for you* (Mark 10:51)?"

No one in this world needs to tell you what you need – you know what you need, and you know it morning, noon, and night.

Jesus is within you. He asks you through the medium of your need and desires, "*What wilt thou that I should do unto thee?*"

Notice that Jesus didn't say to Bartimaeus, "*You now receive your sight; you are now healed.*" Jesus, upon hearing Bartimaeus' desire to receive his sight, said, *"Go thy way; thy faith hath made thee whole"*. Jesus implied via tacit assumption upon the figure of Bartimaeus.

This implied assumption calls the reader to the question, "If Bartimaeus' faith was what made him whole, what was this faith?"

Most respond, "Faith in Jesus, of course," but such an answer is shallow, because it offers no real or practical definition.

Bartimaeus' faith was defined by Jesus in Christ's words found in the following chapter of Mark. It is the faith whereby we not only believe that Jesus exists in the here and now, and we not only believe that Jesus exists within us, but it is also expressed as a discipline that moves us to confront Jesus Christ with our specific needs.

This faith is expressed in the details found within the story. It implies that we believe that He hears us, and this fact demands that we believe immediately upon our expression of need that we have received what we have asked of Him.

Most miss this salient fact: we must, when expressing our desire to Him in prayer, go our way believing that we have received (past tense) what we have asked Him for. It is *upon this complete persuasion that we have received* that we then receive (Mark 11:24). This test reveals the law of assumptive believe, and the subsequent results of its application– this is the defining of the faith that makes man whole.

Notice in the text that it was after Jesus confirmed to Bartimaeus that his faith (his belief that Jesus had given him sight– not "Jesus will in the future give him sight") had made him whole (sight restored).

The tense is critical. The tense is the element that is difficult to understand, and to fully accept, and to apply and maintain.

You and I are, in this art of prayer, commanded to hear the words of Christ (Jesus Christ can and will give us what we desire, which is salvation to us), and to believe (that is to believe that He hears us and is fully competent to perform what we ask of Him), and to repent (From the Greek: Metanoia. A transformative change of the heart), which requires a radical change of thinking regarding our former idea of desire and its position to us, and to be fully immersed within prayer that we have received what we ask of Him.

It is in this respect that we rise from prayer with a new faith that He has answered, and that we have what we have asked of Him. Prayer should, therefore, be viewed as an immersion into the belief of receiving our wish, and coming out of prayer we rise from said immersion.

Bartimaeus was confronted with the Christ. He prayed to receive his sight with the faith that Jesus had the power and the will to save him (restore his sight); therefore, and upon his exercise of faith in Jesus, his sight was restored by his faith, and he went forward following *the way* of Christ.

This is *the way* for you and me today, as it has been since the time of Jesus Christ.

This *way* is not "new thought"– it is the ancient faith described in Hebrews 11. We've missed it, and so it seems new.

Prayer is an art form that requires practice, with its essence being faith in Jesus Christ who is within.

Real prayer requires us to ***live as if*** we already have (past tense) what we've asked Him for in prayer. ***Living as if*** (as if our wish is fulfilled) is the fundamental condition for us to receive (future tense).

Consider this: to ***live as if*** our desire is fulfilled is a concept that requires a level of courage not commonly seen in the modern world.

To *live as if* is seen as *foolishness by the Greeks, and is a stumbling block to the Jews* (1 Cor. 1).

To *live as if* can't be accepted by the natural man. To live as if commands us to believe that we already have what isn't currently seen. Such a belief appears to others as "willful self-deception"– it's utter foolishness to the natural man (2 Cor. 2:14); however, this is *the way.*

I've been a Christian since 1988, and thousands of my prayers have gone unanswered. But I've learned over three decades of trial and error.

This past year I have gained a knowledge and insight that has resulted in miraculous successes in prayer; therefore, it must be passed on to you.

I spent decades praying fervently, seeking real answers to urgent and necessary requests, only to find that my prayers, in most cases, went unanswered.

I saw brothers and sisters in Christ experiencing the same disappointment, discouragement, and bewilderment over unanswered prayers.

I, like you, have seen good people– people who are far better Christians than me, experiencing what appeared to be "silence" from God regarding their prayers.

Well-intentioned people try to encourage the discouraged with sentiments like, "Maybe it wasn't God's will; maybe you asked amiss wanting to spend it on your own lusts; Job lost everything, and he didn't give up".

I agree with their good intentions and sentiments, and I'm familiar with the biblical references. I've said the same things to others.

How could I find the key to prayer?

What's the heart of the matter?

Is it possible to really trust Him?

Is faith just a shot-in-the-dark, and void of real dependency and trust?

Can we truly cast all cares upon Him?

Are the promises of the Bible real?

If I can't depend on Him to answer me, how can I depend on eternal salvation?

These are the questions that are common to all men.

Dear reader, Jesus Christ is real.

The next secret is that He is within you.

You thought that He was somewhere in the sky– in another place, a different realm.

You've been praying to Him in the belief that He is somewhere outside, and above.

The Bible reveals that He is in you.

<u>5</u>

Your Mind: The Garden

For as he thinketh in his heart, so is he.

–King Solomon

Proverbs [23:7; KJV]

All prayer begins in the mind. The mind of man is his garden whereby all is created or destroyed, sustained or extinguished.

Marcus Aurelius said:

"The things you think about determine the quality of your mind. You have power over your mind– not external events. Realize this and you will have strength. Your soul takes on the colour of your thoughts."

It is written of Solomon, *"And God gave Solomon wisdom and understanding exceeding much, and largeness of heart, even as the sand that is on the seashore. And Solomon's wisdom excelled the wisdom of all the children of the east country, and all the wisdom of Egypt. For he was wiser than all men; than Ethan the Ezrahite, and Heman, and Chalcol, and Darda, the sons of Mahol: and his fame was in all nations round about* (1 Kings 4:29-31)".

This same Solomon wrote, *"For as he thinketh in his heart, so is he* (Prov. 23:7)."

You and I become *as we think in our hearts,* and modern scientific methods are finding these ideas to be factual. Neuroscience researcher and scientist,

Dr. Joe Dispenza, was quoted in Wellness & Purpose, (wellnessandpurspose.com) (2019-2024):

> *"It's a scientific fact that the hormones of stress downregulate genes and create diseases and long-term effects. We can think about our problems and turn on those chemicals. That means, though, that our thoughts could make us sick. So, if it's possible that our thoughts can make us sick, is it possible that our thoughts can make us well? The answer is: absolutely yes."*

He further said:

> *"95% of who we are, by the time we are 35 years old, is a memorized set of behaviors, emotional reactions, unconscious habits, hardwired attitudes, beliefs and perceptions, that function like a computer program". It is almost as if most of our reactions are automated, leaving us with just a 5% of our conscious mind to think differently from the mold we have created for ourselves."*

Our thoughts are the sheep of our minds, and they require a shepherd. We are counseled, *"Keep your heart* (mind; core; inner-most being) *with all diligence; for out of it are the issues of life* (Prov. 4:23)."

Jesus said of our heart (mind), *"Are ye also yet without understanding? Do not ye yet understand, that whatsoever entereth in at the mouth goeth into the belly, and is cast out into the draught? But those things which proceed out of the mouth come forth from the heart; and they defile the man. For out of the heart proceed evil thoughts, murders, adulteries, fornications, thefts, false witness, blasphemies: these are the things which defile a man: but to eat with unwashen hands defileth not a man (Matt. 15:16-20)."*

Knowing our minds are a powerfully creative force, we're instructed, *"And be not conformed to this world: but be ye transformed by the renewing of your mind, that ye may prove what is that good, and acceptable, and perfect, will of God (Rom. 12:2)"*.

How do we "renew" our minds? By first remembering that "what we think on habitually" is creating our future (Prov. 23:7); so, with this fact of creation in place, we recognize our need to "weed our gardens".

It may be said that a majority of men have become filled with negative, destructive thoughts; so, their gardens are full of weeds.

This present world's plethora of external influences via television media, print media, and social media act to plant seeds into men's gardens by feeding them a continual mental diet of fear, negativity, lies, perversions, and the like– all are things which act to destroy our minds. It is the act of planting evil and destructive seeds into millions of gardens. We can't allow ourselves to be "conformed" to the world by the seeds it plants in our gardens.

These external influences act as corrosive agents which eat at men's faith in mankind, their hope for the future, their love for life, and their love for their fellow man.

These negative influences are seeds which, when planted in our gardens, will grow into crops that produce a harvest of undesirable fruits which must be destroyed, for such is a fruit of destruction.

This is one reason why the apostle Paul wrote, *"Whatsoever things are true, whatsoever things are honest, whatsoever things are just, whatsoever things are pure, whatsoever things are lovely, whatsoever things are of good report; if there be any virtue, and if there be any praise, think on these things (Phil. 4:8)."*

Such knowledge must not be viewed as "Pollyanna" in nature. This is real, relevant, practical instruction to guard the mind and plant seeds that will produce a future harvest for a life that brings joy, stability, and happiness.

Keep thy heart with all diligence; for out of it are the issues of life (Prov. 4:23) is practical, relevant advice that instructs us to go on a "mental diet".

Weeding your garden requires you to *see what's growing*. Examine your thoughts to see what's been planted. Observe the "mental conversations" you're holding in your mind.

Engaging in self-conversation is a habit that we all indulge in, much like eating and drinking. The key lies not in ceasing this dialogue, but in steering it constructively– because it cannot be stopped. Man can't stop his inner talking no more than he can stop breathing.

Many remain oblivious to the profound impact that these inner conversations have on the circumstances of their lives.

Scripture reminds us, "*As a man thinketh in his heart, so is he*." Do we truly understand that our thoughts create our future? Our thoughts create our paths. We must redirect our paths toward our desired outcomes by shedding our old conversations– our old conversation (behavior) is referred to in the Bible as the old man. We can then be *renewed in the spirit of our minds* (Eph. 4:23).

Our speech (inner dialogue) is a mirror our mind. Our actions are a mirror of our speech. In other words, we act and behave in accord with our inner speech; so, transforming our mind necessitates changing our speech, which will result in a change of behavior.

The world is a realm of endless possible mental transformations, with limitless potential inner conversations. When we uncover the creative power of inner talking, we understand our purpose and mission in life, acting with intention rather than unconsciously.

Every aspect of our life manifests by and through our internal mental conversations we hold in our minds. We, as those who are spiritually enlightened by God's Word, must become conscious of our inner dialogues, and act purposefully.

A person's mental conversations attracts and forms the circumstances of his life. If he does not alter his inner dialogue, his personal story will remain unchanged, and his attempt to transform his world without first changing his inner conversation is futile, as it goes against the natural order.

People can find themselves in repetitive cycles of disappointment, failing to see that their negative inner dialogues are the root cause. Many find comfort in blaming others, but it is their inner dialogues which create their circumstances.

All of this may seem implausible at first, but it is completely verifiable through study and experimentation (testing).

Just as a chemist's formula can be proven, so can the science of transforming words into objective reality.

Consider the story of a young woman who struggled with her boss, convinced that his constant criticisms were unjust. It was explained to her that her perception of him as unfair, and was a sign that she needed to observe her garden, and to create a different inner dialogue. She admitted to "mentally arguing" with her employer every day.

She decided to pray about the circumstance. She changed her inner dialogue. She imagined him praising her work, with her expressing her gratitude for his kindness, in turn. She, in a remarkable turn of events over a period of three days, witnessed a transformation of her boss's behavior toward her, echoing her new inner conversations.

She was *transformed by the renewing of her mind,* and the result was the transformation of her boss's behavior and attitude toward her– her answered prayer! Her outer world transformed to conform with her inner world, and it bore witness to her imaginal activity; therefore, as within, so without.

When I observe people, I often wonder, "What inner conversations are they holding in their minds? What path are they walking?"

Jesus Christ within us seeks to become self-aware in our bodies to fulfill His Father's work. His labor in us involves imitating the Father, mastering the Word, and controlling inner dialogue to shape our world into the likeness of the Kingdom of Love.

Paul urged us to therefore imitate God like dearly loved children (Eph. 5:1, CEV)." How do we imitate God? God calls things that are not as though they were, and they become.

This is how the young woman drew praise and kindness from her employer– by imagining and conversing from a place of fulfillment. She visualized (imagined) the end, which was his praise of her work. Then, she **lived as if** he had already done it, and she remained *in that end* until she witnessed the fulfillment of her desire.

Our inner conversations shape the world we inhabit. Each individual's world is a self-revelation of their inner speech. We are accountable for every idle word we speak, for by our words we are justified or condemned (Matt. 12:36).

Expecting to command life while indulging in negative, destructive, or evil inner talk is foolishness and dangerous. Our present mental conversations don't fade into the past– they project into the future, confronting us as wasted or invested words.

As Isaiah declared, " *So shall my word be that goeth forth out of my mouth: it shall not return unto me void, but it shall accomplish that which I please, and it shall prosper in the thing whereto I sent it* (Isa. 55:11)."

If you want to help a friend or loved one, imagine in prayer that you hear their voice, feeling their presence, and congratulating them on their good fortune. Engage in a loving, knowing communion, believing that your Word sent in love will not return void, but will prosper in its purpose.

"Now is the accepted time, now is the day of salvation (2 Cor. 6:2)." What we do now matters, even if its effects aren't visible until tomorrow. By calling forth creation with intense inner attention, we shape events and relationships in our lives. *As a man thinketh in his heart, so is he.*

We often limit others' willingness and ability to be kind through our fixed attitudes and negative inner dialogues. By consciously creating circumstances through positive inner conversations from the premise of fulfilled desires, we manifest what we wish to see and hear externally.

Our inner conversations are constantly reflected in our surroundings. To see and hear what we desire outwardly, we must first see and hear it "within". Through a disciplined and controlled inner speech aligned with our fulfilled desires, we can set aside all other processes, acting with clear imagination and intention.

Hermes Trismegistus was a legendry Greek figure during the Hellenistic Period who authored a work known as The Hermetica (circa 50-250 AD).

The work recognizes a man's mind and his speech as "divine gifts" which enable man to create the conditions and circumstances of his life.

It is theorized that Trismegistus drew his concepts from the Greek New Testament, as his thoughts reflect John's inspired writings found in John 1, "*In the beginning was the Word, and the Word was with God, and the Word was God. The same was in the beginning with God* (vv. 1-2)."

Mind and Speech are one; thus, transforming our mind transforms our inner conversation.

Paul said, "*That ye put off concerning the former conversation the old man, which is corrupt according to the deceitful lusts; and be renewed in the spirit of your mind; and that ye put on the new man, which after God is created in righteousness and true holiness* (Eph. 4:22-24)".

Changing our inner dialogue, which is the Word of God, is essential for transformation. The prophet Samuel stated, "*The Spirit of the Lord spake by me, and his word was in my tongue* (2 Sam. 23:2)".

Our inner conversations originate in the mind, producing speech movements in the tongue, and these inner conversations are words coming forth from us–

children of God; therefore, we shape and create life as we shape it within ourselves.

Paul said, *"But what saith it? The word is nigh thee, even in thy mouth, and in thy heart: that is, the word of faith, which we preach* (Rom. 10:8)". We are presented with life and death, good and evil, blessings and cursings; let us choose life (Deut. 30:19). The conditions of our lives are not imposed by an external power, but are a result from our freedom to choose our responses.

Now is the time for salvation. Think on things of good report, for your future is shaped by the Word of God– your current inner conversations. You create your future with your inner dialogue. As fields yield crops true to their seeds, so does a man's fate follow his inner speech.

To reap success, we must plant seeds of success within our minds, accepting the truth of our desires through the intensity of our imagination. When the young woman changed her assumption of her employer, his behavior mirrored her new belief.

Persistent assumptions, even if initially false, will solidify into fact. Success demands living wholly in the realm of our assumptive beliefs imagined within prayer– *"believing that we had received what we have asked Him for"*, and holding faithfully to our assumption that we have it (assumptive belief). This is *the way* of Jesus Christ.

External facts may deny your assumptive belief, but your faithful persistence with your vision of the outcome will bring it into reality.

Remember that signs will follow rather than precede (Mark 16:17). Assuming a new concept of oneself is to change inner speech, which may be in one way seen as "putting on a new man". Our unheard inner dialogue shapes our future more than any external promises or threats, so purposefully define your ideal self, and feel the fulfillment of that desire (prayer), trusting that your assumption that you have received what you asked the Lord for will become manifest (Eph. 3:20).

Our faith's true test lies in its application, not its defense. *"And blessed is she that believed: for there shall be a performance of those things which were told her from the Lord* (Luke 1:45)". Test and prove this truth by living in the answer of your desired prayer faithfully.

The world reflects our inner dialogues. Negative inner talk breeds future strife, while positive, loving inner conversations create harmony.

Transforming our mind requires meditating on phrases that imply our ideals are realized, affirming them until they affect us inwardly.

Hold fast to your noble inner convictions, for nothing can take them from you but yourself. All things are generated from your imagination by the Word of God and your inner conversation. Success lies in controlling your inner speech. The price is abandoning the "old man's" conversations and embracing the inner dialogue of the "new man".

Our mind, and the thoughts in our mind, are the gateway to life of our desired state. Fully realizing this reveals the significance of our inner actions. Within our imagining power of our mind, the entire drama of life unfolds repeatedly, and by courageously controlling our inner thoughts and imaginings, we can extend our senses and transform energy from mental and emotional levels to physical reality.

<u>6</u>

The Secret of His Name

The two primary and essential names in the Bible are God (Jehovah) and His Son, Jesus Immanuel Christ (Isa. 7:14; Matt. 1:23). The ancient writers, guided by inspiration of the Holy Spirit, depicted these names through symbolic representations in the language of Hebrew (Old Testament), and Greek (New Testament).

The Hebraic language was a mystical language, because it used symbols to convey deep, esoteric meanings; such meanings were known to the ancient writers, and these meanings have been lost throughout time.

The ancient name of God is written in the Hebraic language as "YHWH", and pronounced in English as "Yahweh" or "Jehovah". This personal name of God is seen in the Hebraic language as "יהוה", and it occurs over 6,800 times in the text.

This Divine name is referred to as the "Tetragrammaton", which means simply "the four letters", and is usually pronounced "Yod-Heh-Waw-Heh" or "Yod-He-Vav-He".

This name of the Hebrew God of the Israelites was first revealed to Moses in the book of Exodus, chapter 3:

"And Moses said unto God, Behold, when I come unto the children of Israel, and shall say unto them, The God of your fathers hath sent me unto you; and they shall say to me, What is his name? what shall I say unto them? And God said unto Moses, I Am That I Am: and he said, Thus shalt thou say unto the children of Israel, I Am hath sent me unto you. And God said moreover unto Moses, Thus shalt thou say unto the children of Israel, the Lord God of your fathers, the God of Abraham, the God of Isaac, and the God of Jacob, hath sent me unto you: this is my name for ever, and this is my memorial unto all generations (Exo. 3:13-15)."

Each consonant in His Divine name is conveyed in a Hebraic symbol as follows:

- Yod– Hand or Seed. This symbol signifies the Hand of the Creator. This is the Power to create, to fashion, to mold, to build within His world.
- Heh– Eye or Window. This second symbol is likened to an eye, or window, which represents the power of

perception; to perceive, insight, spiritual
vision.

- Waw– Nail. Some pronounce the third
  symbol as "Vau" or "Vav". This third
  symbol represents a nail which binds or
  fastens together; it serves as a
  conjunction binding concepts together
  as one.

- Heh– Eye or Window. This fourth
  symbol represents a second eye or
  window, and is said to be the reflective
  projection of creation that was formed
  by the combination of the first three
  symbols, as a projector casts an image
  onto a screen, thus materializing the
  finished creation into reality.

The power of the name of God is paralleled
only by the name of His Son, Jesus Christ, and it is the
secret of His name which gives insight into the secret
of all Creation– and the secret to prayer.

Name means "nature", and the third symbol, Yod (nail), symbolizes the full translation of His name, which means "I AM".

> *And God said unto Moses, I Am That I Am: and he said, Thus shalt thou say unto the children of Israel, I Am hath sent me unto you* (Exo. 3:14).

When you and I say, "I Am", we are pronouncing the name of God– His true and hidden, Divine name. Therefore, when we say, "I AM (and insert a derogatory word, term, or idea)", we are taking His name in vain, for "I AM" is the God of the Bible.

In the most practical terms, Yod represents our awareness, or our "I AM-ness". Therefore, to understand the Great I AM is to understand that He is forever with each one of us through an awareness of our being.

Remember that God is Spirit (Jo. 4:24), God is light (1 Jo. 1:5-7), God is love (1 Jo. 4:16), God is the light of men (Jo. 1:4), God is everywhere in heaven and on earth (Jer. 23:23-24), God is all powerful (2 Tim. 1:7), and God is our consciousness through Jesus Christ within us (Heb. 13:21).

The "Waw" in God's name represents the ability to conceive of and perceive something that is beyond us, and it is the embodiment of the "feeling" of our fulfilled answered prayer– the binding of our desire with the felling of fulfillment of that desire, which is the transformative effect bringing the unseen into the seen (Heb. 11:6).

The last "Heh" in His name reflects our visible, objective world, and our visible world is forever in alignment with our conscious state of being. His Divine name is the foundation of all creation.

We see a demonstrative instruction regarding His name given in Joel:

> *"Beat your plowshares into swords and your pruninghooks into spears:* **let the weak say, I am strong** *(Joel 3:10)."*

Notice that he said to the weak to confess with their mouth, "I am strong". He didn't tell those who were weak, and those who felt physically and mentally weak, to say, "I *will be* strong", but rather "I AM strong"– in spite of feeling weak, or fearful.

Notice the tense: "I AM" is first person, present tense. That is our God. For "*if thou shalt confess with thy mouth the Lord Jesus, and shalt believe in thine heart that God hath raised him from the dead, thou shalt be saved. (Rom. 10:9)"*. We see in Joel that they were to believe, then to confess with their mouths, "I AM strong", and proclaim God's power among the Gentiles toward their salvation.

Prayer is seen as the application and execution of the formula hidden within the very name of God– Yod Heh Waw Heh (YHWH)– the foundation and formula of all creation.

We who are the children of God through faith and baptism into Christ (Gal. 3:26-27), which brought us into adoption as sons through Jesus Christ to Himself (Eph. 1:4-5), find that we are in need. We are confronted with Jesus Christ within, as He asks, *"What do you ask of Me?"*

We, as Bartimaeus, respond in prayer to the Lord with our most urgent need, "Lord, I want to receive my sight!"

We're then confronted with a test of faith. Do I believe that He will save me? In other words, will He give me my desire?

Will we confess our faith that Jesus Christ is within us (2 Cor. 13:5), or will we fail to meet this test as to whether or not we believe, and hold to this faith (*Ibid*)?

We are told to test Him and see, as it is written:

"Bring ye all the tithes into the storehouse, that there may be meat in mine house, and prove me now herewith, saith the Lord of hosts, if I will not open you the windows of heaven, and pour you out a blessing, that there shall not be room enough to receive it (Mal. 3:10)."

Will we accept His invitation? Is He willing and able to restore our sight? Can we muster the courage required to exclaim "Yes, I believe"?

Can we persuade ourselves to the point that we confess, "*I now have received what I have asked of Him*" as is commanded of us by our Lord in Mark 11:24:

*"Therefore, I say unto you, what things soever ye desire, when ye pray, **believe that ye receive them, and ye shall have them.**"*

Believe that you receive them. All answer depends upon this imaginal exercise: I am called to believe that *I have received* what I desire. This is *the way*.

Let's turn to the name of the Son.

The Son's name mirrors the Father's name, as it incorporates the first three Hebraic symbols "Yod Heh Waw". Two additional symbols are added to the Son's name, "Shin Ayin".

As "Yod Heh Waw" is the formulaic sequence of creation, "Hand – Eye – Nail" (power + desire + fastening of the two together), the "Shin" in Jesus' name reveals a remarkable aspect not seen before.

Shin is the symbol of a tooth, or a flame. It is the power to consume and transform, which equates to forgiveness, or that power to detach from and destroy that which is undesirable– forgiveness of our sins.

It was in God's infinite mercy that He brought forth the "Shin" which enables the Son within man to consume or destroy or devour the unlovely and undesirable aspects of our life and world.

It is at this deepest sense that nothing in the Father can cease to exist; however, through the Son we have the ability to be forgiven, thereby transforming us continually and eternally into the likeness of the Son.

These two names of the Father and His Son – secreted from the masses, bestow upon the initiate (the children of God through their obedience to God's plan of eternal salvation), bestow upon each child of God the dominion spoken of in Genesis 1:26-28.

As we walk through this journey of life, we embody these two names and, thereby, create our future reality– as a man thinketh in his heart, so is he (Prov. 23:7). By becoming aware of our righteous desires that will bring us the salvation we so desperately seek, and by bringing forth our desires in prayer to the One Lord Jesus Christ within, and by accepting and believing His instructions to believe that we have received what we have asked Him for, we will receive as He promised (Mark 11:24).

Our prayer answered implies that something was done in consequence of our prayer which otherwise would not have been done; therefore, it can be assumed that our desire was the "main-spring" of action.

It is by the understanding of the name (nature) of the Father and His Son that we find the formulaic mechanism by which prayer is answered.

And it is with this knowledge that we come to the absolute acceptance of why guarding the thoughts (seeds) of our minds (gardens), is so critical.

As you ponder these truths, it is my prayer that you will find the inspiration and courage required to meet the test (2 Cor. 13:5), that you may learn, and implement, and practice this wonderful, secret, hidden art of prayer, so that your every prayer may be answered.

The Bible is not only an ancient manuscript of the factual historical account of God's creation, and revelation of salvation through His Son, Jesus Christ, but beneath the surface of the text are deep phycological meanings that are not commonly understood and taught.

I will reveal some of these deeper meanings in the chapters that follow.

7

Allegory and Meaning

Paul said in Galatians:

"For it is written, that Abraham had two sons, the one by a bondmaid, the other by a freewoman. But he who was of the bondwoman was born after the flesh; but he of the freewoman was by promise. Which things are an allegory: for these are the two covenants; the one from the mount Sinai, which gendereth to bondage, which is Agar (4:22-24)."

The Bible is dual in nature and purpose. The ancient text reveals that the Bible is both a historical record of our Creator and His Son throughout the ages, and it also contains within its allegorical narratives hidden meanings which conceal deep significance that serve to enlighten the children of God throughout time and space.

An allegory is defined as a story, poem, or picture that can be interpreted to reveal a hidden meaning, typically a moral or political one.

Paul said to the Galatians in Galatians 4:24 that the story of Abraham and his two sons are "an allegory"– a story that can be interpreted to reveal a hidden meaning. This implies that certain narratives hold "hidden" meanings.

While some may scoff at this idea, it's written by an apostle. The significance must not be overlooked, for if we take the Bible as a historical document only, the Bible will remain to us as a remote document with limited meaning, and with seeming little practical application to our modern lives.

The ancient story tellers were not only writing history, but they were presenting allegorical scenes–lessons containing specific basic principles draped in the garb of history, and they adapted these stories to the limited mental capacities of the most unsophisticated and unknowing peoples, so that all might come to understand and know the truth.

Unfortunately, many (in my opinion) have mistaken some of the allegories as nothing more than a historical record, and they've taken the "vehicle that conveys instruction" in the limited gross first sense.

In example, we understand that the bread and fruit of the vine (grape juice) is representative of Christ's body and blood; however, some have advocated that the record is a ritual without meaning or application to mankind today.

Others go too far by teaching that the bread and juice transform into real, literal "flesh and blood" after consumption.

The difference between the form of the Bible and its substance is as great as the difference between a mustard seed and the life-germ within that seed. As our internal organs discriminate between food that can be assimilated into our system and food that must be discarded, so do our awakened intuitive faculties discover the phycological life-germ within the allegory.

I'll explain in the pages that follow an allegorical story to try to reveal what the ancient Bible writers intended for us to see, and the phycological truths hidden from the uninitiated.

Here in this text is found the "surface text" of the narrative, or what may be referred to as the gross first sense of the text:

*And Moses went up from the plains of Moab
unto the mountain of Nebo, to the top of
Pisgah, that is over against Jericho. And the
Lord shewed him all the land of Gilead, unto
Dan, And all Naphtali, and the land of
Ephraim, and Manasseh, and all the land of*

Judah, unto the utmost sea, And the south, and the plain of the valley of Jericho, the city of palm trees, unto Zoar. And the Lord said unto him, This is the land which I sware unto Abraham, unto Isaac, and unto Jacob, saying, I will give it unto thy seed: I have caused thee to see it with thine eyes, but thou shalt not go over thither. So Moses the servant of the Lord died there in the land of Moab, according to the word of the Lord. And he buried him in a valley in the land of Moab, over against Bethpeor: but no man knoweth of his sepulchre unto this day (Deut. 34:1-7)."

This historical account of Moses' journey from Moab to Jericho may seem dry on the surface, and quite possibly irrelevant to your life; however, when you become aware of the hidden psychological meaning of this text, your understanding of prayer will be transformed.

When you go to a concordance and search the meaning of the words, then put the words together in sequence, you may be shocked at how this text relates to your prayer, and how it is an allegory of prayer.

Moses. Means to draw out, to rescue, to fetch. Moses is the personification of the power within every man to draw out of the One within (Jesus Christ) that which man needs and seeks, for everything comes from the kingdom within (Luke 17:20-21). Man can receive only what is given from heaven (Jo. 3:27). You draw out from within that which you desire and wish to express as something objective to yourself.

Moab. The contraction of two Hebraic words, "Mem" and "Ab"– meaning Mother-Father. God within you, the Great I AM, works through your consciousness as "Mother and Father", for there is no other cause in your world. God the Father, operating within as both Father and Mother is the Creator that you are always drawing from and out of.

Nebo. Nebo means a prophecy. A prophecy is subjective; in an image of the mind, a subjective desire is "to be", and is not yet a fact. Therefore, the soul must wait and either prove or disprove the prophecy. Nebo is your core desire. It is called a "mountain" because it is the direct challenge before you, and it appears to be difficult to ascend. It is seemingly impossible to overcome and "realize", due to its size and scale. Nebo personifies that which you want to be in contrast to that which you are currently.

Pisgah. Means to contemplate.

Jericho. Means a fragrant odor.

Gilead. Means the hills of witnesses.

Dan. The prophet.

Now bring together the hidden meaning of the text: You are the personification of Moses coming out of the plains of Moab. You examine your core desire (i.e.; I have a desire). My desire appears to be a mountain before me (Nebo).

As I stand here, having now come up from Moab (God within), and having discovered that I can draw out (Moses) from the One within (Jesus Christ), and that He (Jesus) calls me to believe that I have already received my desire (Mark 11:24), I realize that I have within me the One (Jesus) who gives to me all that is required to scale Nebo (my subjective desire).

As I come to the top of Pisgah (to contemplate), I grow close to Jericho (the fragrant odor, which is to sense the answered prayer, or to *feel the success of victory*), as I cannot suppress the joy that comes with the feeling of receiving my answer to my prayer. It is Jericho (fragrant odor of success) that I desire.

And when the Lord brings forth my answer by showing me the land of Gilead (the hills of witnesses)– they, the whole vast world around me, will see that my prayer has been answered. I had presented my alms in secret, and my Father which saw in secret will reward me openly (Matt. 6:4).

This story, as so many others, reveals the hidden secrets to the art of true prayer. You can see the meaning between the gross first sense, or the surface text, and the deeper phycological meaning– the hidden meaning.

This story outlined within a handful of verses in Deuteronomy hides critical components of prayer from the those who are not children of God– the uninitiated.

The next story is of Isaac and his two sons, Esau and Jacob:

> *"And it came to pass, that when Isaac was old,*
> *and his eyes were dim, so that he could not see,*
> *he called Esau his eldest son, and said unto*
> *him, My son: and he said unto him, Behold,*
> *here am I. And he said, Behold now, I am old,*

*I know not the day of my death: Now therefore
take, I pray thee, thy weapons, thy quiver and
thy bow, and go out to the field, and take me
some venison; And make me savoury meat,
such as I love, and bring it to me, that I may
eat; that my soul may bless thee before I die.
And Rebekah heard when Isaac spake to Esau
his son. And Esau went to the field to hunt for
venison, and to bring it. And Rebekah spake
unto Jacob her son, saying, Behold, I heard thy
father speak unto Esau thy brother, saying,
Bring me venison, and make me savoury meat,
that I may eat, and bless thee before
the Lord before my death. Now therefore, my
son, obey my voice according to that which I
command thee. Go now to the flock, and fetch
me from thence two good kids of the goats; and
I will make them savoury meat for thy father,
such as he loveth: And thou shalt bring it to thy
father, that he may eat, and that he may bless
thee before his death. And Jacob said to
Rebekah his mother, Behold, Esau my brother
is a hairy man, and I am a smooth man: My
father peradventure will feel me, and I shall*

seem to him as a deceiver; and I shall bring a curse upon me, and not a blessing. And his mother said unto him, Upon me be thy curse, my son: only obey my voice, and go fetch me them. And he went, and fetched, and brought them to his mother: and his mother made savoury meat, such as his father loved. And Rebekah took goodly raiment of her eldest son Esau, which were with her in the house, and put them upon Jacob her younger son: And she put the skins of the kids of the goats upon his hands, and upon the smooth of his neck: And she gave the savoury meat and the bread, which she had prepared, into the hand of her son Jacob. And he came unto his father, and said, My father: and he said, Here am I; who art thou, my son? And Jacob said unto his father, I am Esau thy first born; I have done according as thou badest me: arise, I pray thee, sit and eat of my venison, that thy soul may bless me. And Isaac said unto his son, How is it that thou hast found it so quickly, my son? And he said, Because the Lord thy God brought it to me. And Isaac said unto Jacob, Come near, I pray thee, that I may feel thee, my son, whether thou be my very son Esau or not. And Jacob went near unto Isaac his father; and he felt him, and said, The voice is Jacob's voice, but the hands are the hands of Esau. And he discerned him not, because his hands were hairy, as his brother Esau's hands: so, he blessed him. And he said, Art thou my very son Esau? And he said, I am. And he said, Bring it near to me, and I will eat of my son's venison, that my soul may bless thee. And he brought it near to him, and he did eat: and he brought him wine and he drank. And his father Isaac said unto him, Come near now, and kiss me, my son. And he came near, and kissed him: and he smelled the smell of his raiment, and blessed him, and said, See, the smell of my son is as the smell of a field which the Lord hath blessed: Therefore God give thee of the dew of heaven, and the fatness of the earth, and plenty of corn and wine: Let people serve thee, and nations bow down to thee: be lord over thy brethren, and let thy mother's sons bow down to thee: cursed be every one that curseth thee, and

blessed be he that blesseth thee. And it came to
pass, as soon as Isaac had made an end of
blessing Jacob, and Jacob was yet scarce gone
out from the presence of Isaac his father, that
Esau his brother came in from his hunting.
And he also had made savoury meat, and
brought it unto his father, and said unto his
father, Let my father arise, and eat of his son's
venison, that thy soul may bless me. And Isaac
his father said unto him, Who art thou? And he
said, I am thy son, thy firstborn Esau. And
Isaac trembled very exceedingly, and said,
Who? where is he that hath taken venison, and
brought it me, and I have eaten of all before
thou camest, and have blessed him? yea, and
he shall be blessed. And when Esau heard the
words of his father, he cried with a great and
exceeding bitter cry, and said unto his father,
Bless me, even me also, O my father.
And he said, Thy brother came with subtilty,
and hath taken away thy blessing. And he said,
Is not he rightly named Jacob? for he hath
supplanted me these two times: he took away
my birthright; and behold, now he hath taken

away my blessing. And he said, Hast thou not reserved a blessing for me? And Isaac answered and said unto Esau, Behold, I have made him thy lord, and all his brethren have I given to him for servants; and with corn and wine have I sustained him: and what shall I do now unto thee, my son? And Esau said unto his father, Hast thou but one blessing, my father? bless me, even me also, O my father. And Esau lifted up his voice, and wept. And Isaac his father answered and said unto him, Behold, thy dwelling shall be the fatness of the earth, and of the dew of heaven from above; And by thy sword shalt thou live, and shalt serve thy brother; and it shall come to pass when thou shalt have the dominion, that thou shalt break his yoke from off thy neck (Genesis 27:1-40)."

Here is the explicit picture of a blind man being deceived by his second son into giving him a blessing which belonged to the first son.

The story stresses the point that deception was accomplished through two human senses: touch and smell. Isaac's blindness indicates that a lack of sight is present, as well.

This story is a comparative allegory hiding the elements of successful prayer for men throughout the ages, and its hidden elements should be re-enacted and applied as a technique for prayer. Yes, this sounds bizarre, but give me the latitude and love to explain what is meant.

You are as the blind Isaac, and you have two allegorical sons– the hairy outer man (carnal man), Esau, and the smooth-skinned inner man (your spiritual being), Jacob.

You, as Isaac, enter prayer as you close your sight to all outer images and senses. This is what is meant by Christ's words in Matthew 6:6, *"But thou, when thou prayest, enter into thy closet, and when thou hast shut thy door, pray to thy Father which is in secret; and thy Father which seeth in secret shall reward thee openly"*.

As you enter into your closet and shut the door behind, you are closing yourself off to all external senses– you are now blind.

You meet your Father in this "place within".

You have sent away your son, Esau– the outer man. This means that you have taken your focus away from all outer senses, and you begin to pray which removes your consciousness from Easu.

The second son, Jacob, represents your inner ma– your spiritual being. He holds your desire.

It is this inner man who seeks to be blessed by his Father. It is this inner man who desires to "supplant", or to take the place of, the outer, carnal man.

Your inner man overhears the gift of the Father – the birthright. Jacob desires the birthright– the blessing of the Father.

Jacob disguises himself as the outer man. This refers to giving "feeling" to your desire, as Isaac uses the feeling of touch and smell to bless Jacob.

We, within our prayer, present our desire. We, through the engagement and exercise of our imaginal faculty, begin to imagine that we touch and smell our desire. We make it real from within via imagination.

As we make our desire a reality, the Father touches and smells the "reality"– he accepts that the inner desire is the outer reality and, thereby, passes the blessing.

We obey Christ's command, *"Believe that you have received it"*. How do we obey His command? We ***feel as if*** we have the answer.

To accomplish this feeling, we ask ourself, "What would it feel to receive the answer?" As we imagine the feeling of the wish fulfilled, we begin to marry our imaginal act to the accompanying emotion. This "marrying" brings forth the creative act.

It is written in Acts 17:27:

*"That they should seek the Lord, if haply they might **feel after him**, and find him, though he be not far from every one of us."*

It is through the sense of feeling that we come to accept Christ's instruction to *"believe that you have received* (Mark 11:24)," for "feeling" is a critical and secret element of successful prayer.

Smell was the second sense seen in the story. Using smell in this way is the method of bringing tones of reality to our answered prayer.

In example, if I ask you to close your eyes and visualize a rose under your nose, you can smell the rose after a few seconds, in spite of the fact that no rose exists at this moment under your nose. Try it and you'll experience the truth of this exercise.

It is in these applied practices that we assist ourselves in persuading ourselves that we have realized our answered prayer.

Isaac said, "*Come near, I pray thee, that I may feel thee, my son, whether thou be my very son Esau or not (Gen. 27:21)*". *And Isaac said to Jacob, "Come near now, and kiss me, my son. And he came near, and kissed him: and he smelled the smell of his raiment, and blessed him, and said, See, the smell of my son is as the smell of a field which the Lord hath blessed (Gen. 27:26-27)*".

It was at this point that Isaac pronounced the blessing on Jacob.

Verse 30 says, "*And it came to pass, as soon as Isaac had made an end of blessing Jacob, and Jacob was yet scarce gone out from the presence of Isaac his father, that Esau his brother came in from his hunting.*" The hidden meaning represents your awareness as you come out of your prayer. The outer man, Esau, returns from the hunt quickly after you feel the blessing of your answered prayer. Esau is the return of your outer man into the outer physical world.

Don't become anxious in this practical approach, for it is your Father's good pleasure to give you the kingdom (Luke 12:32) that is within (Luke 17:21).

Consider the practical approach:

You rest comfortably in a quiet, secluded room, and you close your eyes. Relax and slow your breathing. Remove all focus from the outer room, and your physical being.

Your inner being, Jacob, seeks God's blessings, so you make your desires known to the Father in prayer.

Jesus within you calls upon you to believe that you have received what you ask for.

Now, with all of this in mind, begin to "feel" the feeling of having received the answer. Add tones of reality to the answer– hear what the answer sounds like, and smell what you would smell if your prayer was answered.

You are bringing your desired future into the here and now, and you are doing so to the point that your objective is so close that you can "feel it".

Can you remain faithful to your belief that your prayer is answered, and that you have what you asked for that you will receive it as Jesus said?

Isaac, in this story, could not retract the blessing, in spite of the fact that the blessing had been given through deceit.

When you pray using the elements of this story as instructive methods, the Father will not retract his blessings– but you must remain faithful to His promise.

Remaining faithful means that you must control the thoughts of your mind. Your thoughts are sheep, and you are the shepherd. Your effort to develop the mind of Christ is to make the Good Shepherd the shepherd of your thoughts. We make the continual conscious effort to mold and shape our every thought into a pure, loving though based on faith, which is to shepherd our thoughts through the lens of Jesus Christ. In this way we are *letting this mind be in us, which was also in Christ Jesus* (Phil. 2:5).

You must, at every moment of the day, reject all negative thoughts of doubt, and worry, and fear. You must eradicate every such negative thought by faith that the Father has heard your petition, and that you have received your answer as promised by Jesus Christ.

Remaining faithful to the outcome is to allow the seed to sprout, to grow, and to meet your harvest in the near future.

"*And Jesus said unto them, Because of your unbelief: for verily I say unto you, If ye have faith as a grain of mustard seed, ye shall say unto this mountain, Remove hence to yonder place; and it shall remove; and nothing shall be impossible unto you* (Matt. 17:20)."

Remaining faithful to the outcome can also be seen in our Lord's instructions found in Revelation 2:10, "*Fear none of those things which thou shalt suffer: behold, the devil shall cast some of you into prison, that ye may be tried; and ye shall have tribulation ten days: be thou faithful unto death, and I will give thee a crown of life.*"

While we realize that our Lord is speaking of death in the sense of the death of our life on this earth, and receiving the crown of eternal life with Him in Heaven, this may also apply to our faithfulness to His promises regarding prayer, as He is speaking of the trials and tribulations that we face in this life in the here and now. We're to ignore the external conditions and to hold fast to our desired outcome that we asked for in prayer. This is what it means to "live in the end".

If we can muster the courage to live in the end– that is, to live as if our prayer is already answered, and maintain that state of being without turning back, we will, in short order, be crowned with the life that we desire.

Your faith will make you whole.

8
Assumptive Belief

I was baptized into the Lord and His kingdom in 1988, and I can testify that this journey has been filled with the joys of following in the way; but I've also experienced my fair share of failure and tribulation.

This statement is not to illicit sympathy. It's an effort to be transparent, and to admit that my failures are my own.

The purpose of sharing this book is two-fold: 1) The primary purpose is to provide the Lord's people with insight that they might not otherwise have, in a genuine effort to truly help, and encourage, and to edify God's people. 2) The second purpose to give to you the underlying meaning of the text in the hope that you will find the courage to test the principles and ideas herein that you may live the more abundant life in Christ.

Christ's crucifixion was the ultimate gift of God to mankind, and the good news is that all men can obtain eternal life through Jesus Christ.

Paul outlined the good news, or gospel, in 1 Corinthians 15:

> *Moreover, brethren, I declare unto you the gospel which I preached unto you, which also*

*ye have received, and wherein ye stand; By
which also ye are saved, if ye keep in memory
what I preached unto you, unless ye have
believed in vain. For I delivered unto you first
of all that which I also received, how that
Christ died for our sins according to the
scriptures; And that he was buried, and that he
rose again the third day according to the
scriptures: And that he was seen of Cephas,
then of the twelve: After that, he was seen of
above five hundred brethren at once; of whom
the greater part remain unto this present, but
some are fallen asleep. After that, he was seen
of James; then of all the apostles* (vv. 1-7).

Our response to the gospel that we may receive
forgiveness of sins is made clear throughout the remote
text of the New Testament, and is set forth by the
Spirit's inspired instructions to hear the gospel (Rom.
10:17), and to believe it (Jo. 3:16), to repent of sin
(Luke 13:3), to confess our belief in Jesus Christ as the
Son of God and do so publicly (Romans 10:9-11), to
be baptized into Jesus for the remission of sins (Acts
2:38; 1 Peter 3:21), and to remain steadfast and faithful

until death so that we may receive the crown of everlasting life (Revelation 2:10).

The instructions and examples are set forth clearly within the pages of the New Testament.

Why do I outline the plan of salvation for mankind in a book about prayer? The reason is because the New Testament teaches that spiritual blessings are enjoyed *in Christ*, as it is written, *"Blessed be the God and Father of our Lord Jesus Christ, who hath blessed us with all spiritual blessings in heavenly places in Christ"* (Eph. 1:3). So, the starting point is not prayer – it is to get into Christ. How?

> *"Therefore, we are buried with him by baptism into death: that like as Christ was raised up from the dead by the glory of the Father, even so we also should walk in newness of life (Rom. 6:4)."*

I witnessed, after getting into Christ, prayers in every form from the pulpit, during the Lord's Supper, at functions, events, in Christian's homes, etc.; however, I was never *taught* to pray, or how to pray, or what to expect, or anything related to prayer.

In thirty-plus years of attending worship services, I can think of only a handful of sermons on prayer. Generally, the sermons were on the model prayer called the Lord's prayer, or usually limited to that.

This is in no way a finding of fault in teachers or preachers or others… its merely an observational fact. So, we seem to learn about prayer entirely on our own, for the most part. We stumble and grope through the mechanics of prayer as we've heard them from others. Our expectations are uncertain and, quite possibly, inaccurate.

I admit that in this thirty-plus-year-span of "trial and error of prayer", it's been a roller-coaster ride. I've met with preachers, deacons, elders, and others regarding my confusion and struggles and incorrect expectations relating to my prayers.

I, like you, have seen countless others pray during dire straits within urgent needs, only to see many suffer disappointment and discouragement.

Disappointments are usually met with well-meaning statements like, "It was God's will; don't give up – just keep the faith; God knows best; He hears you, so don't be angry with Him, just accept His decision, maybe you asked amiss, etc."

This statement regarding "to ask amiss" finds its origin in James 4:3:

"Ye ask, and receive not, because ye ask amiss, that ye may consume it upon your lusts."

Understand that I am well aware of the principles of this verse, and I am completely aware that some ask for inappropriate things – but this verse is not applicable, relevant, or meaningful to most of those who find themselves continually discouraged by unanswered prayers, as most (in my experience), didn't ask for something that they could consume upon their own lusts.

We also recognize that there are some who think that they can become rich, famous, and powerful through prayer. Paul told Timothy:

"Holding faith, and a good conscience; which some having put away concerning faith have made shipwreck: Of whom is Hymenaeus and Alexander; whom I have delivered unto Satan, that they may learn not to blaspheme (1 Tim. 1:19-20)."

Paul said in chapter 6 of the same letter: *"But they that will be rich fall into temptation and a snare, and into many foolish and hurtful lusts, which drown men in destruction and perdition. For the love of money is the root of all evil: which while some coveted after, they have erred from the faith, and pierced themselves through with many sorrows* (1 Tim. 6:9-10)."

It is my belief that most sincere Bible students know these truths, and this book assumes that the reader knows that the author is not implying riches or fame through prayer.

At the same time, it must be stated in truth that if a man or woman desires provision, or blessings to provide for and pass to children and grandchildren, these desires are not only common, but they are righteous and holy.

Solomon said, *"House and riches are the inheritance of fathers: and a prudent wife is from the Lord* (Prov. 19:14)."

What right-thinking man doesn't want to provide an inheritance to his children? And what right-thinking man doesn't want good, prudent wife?

We recognize that riches and honor come from the Lord, as the Chronicler wrote, *"Both riches and honour come of thee, and thou reignest over all; and in thine hand is power and might; and in thine hand it is to make great, and to give strength unto all* (1 Chron. 29:12)."

The point is simple: *every good and perfect gift is from above, and cometh down from the father of lights, with whom is no variableness, neither shadow of turning* (James 1:17).

In the summer of 1983, and at the tender age of sixteen, I prayed for a wife. Yes, a wife. At sixteen. Crazy, right?

I remember kneeling in prayer at the foot of my water-bed (it was 1983), praying to God that someday He would give me a good wife.

Why? Because I didn't want to experience the divorces I'd seen in my own family. I figured that if I started to pray early– at the age of sixteen, then He might find me a wife by the time I was out of college. I wanted to give Him plenty of time.

In October of that same year, just a few months later, I met Jonetta. We were married in '85, and we've been together ever since. God answered that prayer quickly.

I have no recollection of how I "felt" after that prayer, or that I believed that the prayer would be answered.

I do remember that I said, "God, it's in your hands", and I forgot about it. I released the seed into the garden and didn't disturb it.

In June of 1985, a month before our wedding, I told Jonetta that I wanted to find a computer job in Nashville, and that I had prayed to have it. I knew without a doubt that God would answer that prayer, in spite of the fact that I was just eighteen years old, with no training, no education, no background, no family or social connections, and no resources– but somehow, I knew that He'd answer that prayer.

In February of 1986, I was working for a pest control company called Cook's Pest Control based out of Decatur, Alabama, and trying to attend college at night.

My bug-route included a section of Nashville known as Green Hills. On a cold day in February, I was doing a spider-treatment in a very nice home in Green Hills. The older female customer instructed me to go to her second-floor, as her son had an apartment upstairs, and she wanted me to spray for spiders up there, as well.

I knocked on the second-floor apartment door, and Scott opened the door– he'd stopped at home during his lunch hour.

Scott was a young handsome Jewish man who was educated, well-spoken, and incredibly charismatic. We began to talk as I sprayed the apartment, and I asked what he did for a living. He replied that he worked for a company called OSI Data Solutions, and explained that they were a large regional dealer of high-end printing equipment, offset presses, cameras, computer printers, fax machines, patient admissions systems used by major hospitals, and computer-identification badging systems.

I replied enthusiastically that I want to work for a computer company.

"Mike, we're hiring right now. How about I see if I can introduce you to some of our management staff, and get you an interview?"

Scott arranged the interview, introduced me to upper management, and I was hired in March of 1986– a month before my nineteenth birthday.

That happened eight months after I had prayed for a Nashville computer job.

That company and job was the one that I wrote about in Muscle and a Shovel.

Scott and I maintain a close friendship to this day, and he and his wife still live in Nashville.

Successful prayer.

God answers prayer. Even when we don't know what we're doing, God answers our prayers.

Throughout my life I can trace my successful prayers to my confidence that God would, without any shadow of a doubt and in spite of all odds, answer my prayer in the affirmative.

Fast forward to December 2018: the economy in southern Illinois was suffering, and Jonetta and I were spiritually stagnant. Ideas for writing were non-existent, and we both longed to be in the Rocky Mountains. Our Metropolis home had been listed for sale for almost two years at that point, with no offers. Dozens had looked at our home, but no offers were ever made. The home was priced at $275k, and it was one of the most expensive homes in the county.

No one seemed to be able to afford it, so we took it off the market. There was no longer any hope of a move to the mountains. We'd given up– we would stay in and retire in and die in southern Illinois.

In the early morning hours of February of 2019, I walked to my back-yard cabin with a cup of coffee in hand and I stopped dead in my tracks.

"*We're leaving.*" The thought came from the deep desire of my heart.

"*Yes, we're leaving. We're going to the mountains. It's what she wants. It's what I want.*"

I opened the cabin door and got on my knees…

Within that prayer in the quiet of my cabin, I "*felt it*". I felt the cool mountain air– I actually smelled it. I felt the breeze on my face while visualizing Pike's Peak.

"Jonetta, we're going," I said in a rush coming through the back door of the house.

"Going where?" she said in surprise at the conviction in my voice.

"Colorado," I said while taking a seat at her desk.

She laughed. "Have you lost your mind? We can't sell this hou–"

"It doesn't matter," I interrupted.

"It does matter, Michael! We can't afford to leave!"

"Listen, I know it sounds crazy, but we're going," I said as I slowed the pace of our conversation. "I don't know how– I just know we're going."

I had "felt" the answer in that prayer.

Four days later we landed at DIA. We drove to Castle Rock and got a hotel room. The following morning, Jonetta had the laptop open.

"Rentals are going as soon as they're listed," she said as she worked the keyboard. "I don't see how we're going to be able to get a house as fast as these are renting."

"Keep looking and I'll go down and get us some coffee," I responded, and left the room.

My phone buzzed when I got to the lobby.

"I found a house in the Springs," she talked fast, "but we've got to go now! The realtor has another couple looking at the house in an hour."

I checked my watch. It would take us almost an hour to get to Colorado Springs from Castle Rock.

"Grab my coat and meet me in the lobby."

We rented the house on the spot, and it was terrifying. Here we were in Colorado. We'd just signed an expensive lease on a home, but we still had a mortgage on a home back in Illinois that wasn't even on the market– a home we'd tried our best to sell, and it wouldn't sell.

How was this going to work? I didn't need to know. I'd prayed and somehow knew He would answer.

We landed in St. Louis and was on our way back to Metropolis.

"What are we going to do?" asked Jonetta. It was a fair question. I didn't have an answer.

"Pray."

"Pray for–"

"Pray we sell the house," I interrupted.

We must sell the house. There's no other option. I felt this in my prayer. This will work. God will make a way...

The next morning, I was puttering through the backyard toward the cabin, making tracks in the snow... my phone rang.

"Michael, this is Kim." She was our old realtor.

"Hi, Kim."

"You remember that couple from Indiana that looked at your home last year…"

Incredibly, Kim had received a call that morning from a couple who had looked at our home a year before. They liked the home but said it wasn't a good fit for them.

The house had been off the market for a long time at that point, and we'd never had a single offer from a buyer during the long stretch that it was listed for sale. There was no good reason for us to believe that we would sell the house. These conditions were the facts.

Our logical mind is steeped in the reasons and facts why a thing can't be done. Our mind examines the facts and concludes the impossibility.

To assume in impossible outcome which is in opposition to the facts is unreasonable, unsound thinking, and utter foolishness.

This kind of foolishness is *the way*.

It was foolish for Bartimaeus to believe that a man called Jesus could restore his sight– but his faith made him whole.

Within seven days of our return from Colorado, and after having signed a lease on another home, and with no "visible" way to sell our home in Illinois, the impossible was brought into reality. The Lord answered our prayer. I had, within and during that prayer, felt and smelled the answer.

All of my decisions after prayer were directed and based upon my assumption that my prayer had already been answered.

I *lived as if*. I *lived in the end*– the end of the prayer.

More importantly, this event and the subsequent answer was the first time that I was able to connect my actions to Mark 11:24. This is a primary key.

Blind trust.

Stupidity? Foolishness? Actions of an unsound mind?

This is *the way– His way*. The way seems like foolishness to the Greeks, and it is a stumbling block to the Jews (1 Cor. 1:23-25).

Has He answered every prayer? No. I'm sorry to say that He has not– not in the way that I wanted, and not in the way that I can yet see.

Have I been discouraged? Absolutely.

Have I always been able to feel and smell and touch and been fully persuaded that I have received what I have asked before it came into being, as Jesus taught in Mark 11:24? No, I have not, and therein lies the cause of unanswered prayer.

I firmly assert via personal, direct, multiple experiences in prayer, and witnessing the results– whether positive or negative, that Jesus Christ's words found in Mark 11:24 are absolutely true, and can be depended upon.

I will also freely admit that His teaching requires great courage for full acceptance, and the maintenance of bold courage to remain faithful to the outcome– the belief that you have already received what you asked for, and a childlike faith to dispel all anxiety, doubt, and disbelief.

The hidden art of prayer requires a courage unseen in the modern world. When all of the external forces are acting as witnesses in bringing you to an undesirable and even tragic end, bold courage and a childlike faith is required.

For those who accept the challenge and test this principle– if they can ignore and repel and refute all external evidence, and if they can hold to their vision of their desired outcome which was "felt" within their prayer, they will have what they have asked for according to His promise.

I can attest to my numerous prayers that have been answered– many of which seemed absolutely impossible.

They were– and I hesitate to use this word… miracles.

To me, and in view of the impossibility of realizing the answer that I demanded of God, you would call them miracles, too.

Yes, we know that the "Age of Miracles" ended in the first century, but what else can we call such results?

I simply do not know.

<u>2</u>
Siloed

Christians run the risk becoming siloed. Siloed means to enter or fall into a state of isolation, or separation in a way that hinders or prevents additional information, communication, and cooperation.

In our well-intentioned efforts to *stand ye in the ways and see, and ask for the old paths where is the good way and walk therein* (Jer. 6:16), we create an automatic mental mechanism that completely rejects any information that doesn't immediately fit within the mental framework of our traditional, orthodox views.

This is siloed.

"Is the information from a member of the church? Is the information presented in ways that fit my definition of sound teaching? Is the one presenting the information a 'true Christian'? Will my examination of the information risk my position and status– will I be labeled unfaithful, unsound, or a heretic?"

We must, of course, contend for the faith (Jude 1:3). We must hold fast to sound teaching (2 Tim. 1:13-14). We must not heap unto ourselves teachers, having itching ears (2 Tim. 4:3-4). We must not turn away our ears from the truth, and be turned unto fables (*Ibid*).

In the framework of these truths, we must employ our understanding of the scriptures with our God-given discernment to receive information with readiness of mind, and then to search the scriptures to see if what we hear is actually so (Acts 17:11).

This attitude of mind will allow us to consider what we might deem as "new or different" information, but at the same time protect our hearts and minds and faith by searching the scriptures and comparing what we've heard to the Word, so that we may know without a doubt if it is so.

Contending for this wonderful faith of Jesus Christ is a warning and command of the scriptures (Jude 1:3), and I take this instruction as it is presented, and with the seriousness and urgency it deserves.

I also realize that there is a severe risk in presenting ancient concepts from the scriptures that may, at first, appear as "new" or "unorthodox".

However, I've been there before.

Discovering the meaning and purpose of baptism into Christ was for me, some thirty-plus years ago, very new and unorthodox– but thanks be to God that I was willing to at least consider the text and the meanings thereof.

In 2020, I stumbled onto a YouTube video by Gregg Braden. Gregg's bio says that he is a five-time New York Times best-selling author, scientist, educator and pioneer in the emerging paradigm bridging science, social policy and human potential.

The title of the video caught my attention: *"Gregg Braden – Be Enveloped by What You Desire – Jesus on Praying in Aramaic Gospel & Gospel of Thomas."* Gregg discusses how he visited an Egyptian Monastery and reviewed an ancient text called the Gospel of Thomas. I'll stop here and qualify my statements by saying that I do not believe that the Gospel of Thomas is inspired, nor am I advocating the book. I'm merely sharing this information to bring you to a biblical point in the pages following.

Gregg said that he viewed this ancient text translated from the NAG Hammadi library, and in verse 106 it says, "When you make the two, thought and emotion, become one– when you make the two 'one' [within your mind and heart], you will say to the mountain, 'Move away,' and the mountain will move away; when thought and emotion become one, the feeling [power] is created in our body."

Gregg then brings up John 16:23-24, and discusses that the current King James Version reveals an "edited" version, as two sentences found in the original Aramaic were removed in the KJV during the fourth century. The KJV text he's speaking of is in John 16:23-24:

And in that day ye shall ask me nothing. Verily, verily, I say unto you, Whatsoever ye shall ask the Father in my name, he will give it you. Hitherto have ye asked nothing in my name: ask, and ye shall receive, that your joy may be full.

Gregg then shows his audience what was removed by the KJV translators:

"Ask without hidden motive and be surrounded by your answer. Be enveloped by what you desire, that your gladness be full[1].

Gregg discusses the idea that there is a "field of Divine matrix" whereby everything is created,

---

1. Text alleged to have been removed from the KJV in the fourth century. Gregg Braden, YouTube, 2020. From Prayers of the Cosmos: Meditations on the Aramaic Words of Jesus, Neil Douglas-Klotz, pp. 86-87; Secrets of the Lost Mode of Prayer: The Hidden Power of Beauty, Blessing, Wisdom, and Hurt, Gregg Braden, pp. 166-167

and that we must "speak to the field in a language that the field understands".

He explains that, according to his understanding, the "field" understands the "feelings created within the heart– not words of speech, but feelings created by our marrying together of the two components, thought and emotion, which create the "feeling" that the "field" understands and acts upon.

It is in the execution of this practice, according to Gregg, that we are "surrounded by our answer" and, therefore, empowers the field to act in the fulfillment of our desire that our gladness may be full.

Regarding Gregg's statement in reference to Christ's words, "*Hitherto have ye asked nothing in my name* (John 16:24)," he explains that the meaning of this phrase "*ye have asked nothing in my name*" was revealed in the text that was removed by the King James translators. "*To ask in his name*" means "*to ask without hidden motive and to be surrounded by your answer – be enveloped by what you desire*".

He goes on, "To ask in his name does not mean to 'speak a word'– it means to be surrounded in your answer. If you are surrounded in your answer, you are feeling as if your answer has already happened."

"Be enveloped if you want the perfect relationship in your life. If you want the healing in the body of your loved ones, feel the feeling of what it is like as if that has already happened. Be enveloped by what you desire, because that is when your thought and your emotion are married together and become 'one'.

"You think the thought of the healing in your loved ones, and you feel the love of that thought. The thought and feeling become one – this is the language that this field recognizes.

"Ask without hidden motive. What does that mean? To ask without judgment. This is precisely what the Buddhists are telling us– ask without the judgment of the right or the wrong or the good or the bad. Ask without the ego. Ask from the heart.

"To be surrounded means to 'feel as if' [as if your prayer is already answered].

Gregg continues, "We spoke this morning about Neville[2], the philosopher Neville early in the 20th

---

2. Neville Goddard, The Power of Awareness, 1952.

century in his book *The Power of Awareness*. Look at what he says– it's the same thing. Neville says you must make your future dream a present fact now by assuming the feeling of your wish fulfilled. To come from the place that it's already happened.

"Now this is what those practitioners did [healed] with that cancerous tumor."

Let's bring forth the text of John 16 again:

And in that day ye shall ask me nothing. Verily, verily, I say unto you, Whatsoever ye shall ask the Father in my name, he will give it you. Hitherto have ye asked nothing in my name: ask, and ye shall receive, that your joy may be full.

The facts that we can confirm are:
1. Jesus begins with the emphatic, twice repeated, *"Verily"*.

    i. *"Verily"*, from the Greek " ἀμήν ". Meaning: Truly; amen; of a truth; most assuredly; so, let it be.

    ii. This word, when used, notified the listener that an emphatic and settled truth would soon follow.

2. Jesus admonished them that *whatsoever* they asked the Father in His name, the Father would give it to them.

    i.   This was the promise made by Jesus regarding prayer.

    ii.   The promise establishes the bar of unconditioned and unlimited expectation in the petitioner.

    iii.   "*Whatsoever*", from the Greek " τι ". Meaning: Any; anything; in any way; without judgment; unconditioned; without limit; without motive.

3. Jesus revealed concern for the disciple's existing misunderstanding and incorrect methodology unto that moment in time, as proven by His statement, "*Hitherto have ye asked nothing in my name.*"

    i.   The standard is thereby set forth: all petitions must be asked in His name.

4. Jesus reiterates the promise and provides
the reason via admonishment, *"ask, and ye
shall receive, that your joy may be full.*

   i. He commands them to *"ask"*.

   ii. He establishes expectations, *"and ye
shall receive"*.

   iii. He reveals the reason behind His
promise, *"that your joy may be full."*

The foregoing facts make plain His promise, His methodology, our expectations, and His motive–that we receive so that our joy may be made full.

We now find, according to Braden, that a portion of Christ's words were, quite possibly, removed from the translation and suppressed from public consumption. The missing portions are, again:

"Ask without hidden motive and be surrounded by your answer. Be enveloped by what you desire, that your gladness be full.

If this is true, then additional facts to be included are as follows:

1. Jesus instructs to *ask without hidden motive.*

i.   Jesus established in John 16:23 that
no limit would be placed upon the
Father's ability by His use of the
word, "*Whatsoever*".

ii.   Jesus then removes all restriction
from His petitioner's by His use of
the words, "*hidden motive*",
meaning, quite possibly, that the
petitioner was not to engage in
"conditioning" or qualifying his
petition via unspoken personal
judgment.

2. Jesus instructs to *be surrounded by your answer*.

i.   The implication is that "*answer*"
means "desired outcome", as proven
in His statement that follows.

3. Jesus further instructs and explains, "*Be enveloped by what you desire*".

i.   Reason and logic draw all to
conclude that Jesus' use of the word
"surrounded" in the first statement
conveys the same meaning as the
second word "enveloped"; likewise,

we see the same in His use of the
words "answer" and "desire".

IF the words of John 16 are true as we believe they are, and IF this newly discovered information– the information that what was discovered are Christ's words in the original Aramaic from the fourth century that were removed or suppressed or censored by the King James Version translators– if this information is true, this information reveals a more complete method of prayer from the Master.

Don't get anxious or critical, as I am not stating that the information is or is not authentic. I am saying that IF the Aramaic text is authentic, it may be the textual documentation which verifies these concepts.

Why would those commissioned to translate the KJV omit this critical information? I admit that I have strong personal opinions that I will not discuss herein.

My purpose is to reveal the information and encourage you to judge with righteous (right-thinking) judgment (Jo. 7:24) for yourself.

10

Test Yourself

The realization that Jesus and His kingdom is within you (Luke 17:21; 1 Cor. 13:6) can be shocking, as many Christians still believe Him to be in a far off place. Knowing that Jesus in us is our hope of glory, as Paul wrote:

> *"To whom God would make known what is the riches of the glory of this mystery among the Gentiles; **which is Christ in you, the hope of glory** (Col. 1:27)."*

Christ in you– the hope of glory (Col. 1:27), and *that Christ may dwell in your hearts by faith* (Eph. 3:17).

The word heart is from the Greek, "kardia", and means, "the mind; the inner self"; therefore, He dwells within you at your inner core. He dwells within your skull – in your mind (Phil. 2:5), which is within your skull.

This is the psychological meaning of Golgotha (from the ancient Greek: Golgotha. Skull). The crucifixion at Calvary conveys the psychological meaning of the skull (from the Latin: a Skull).

Paul told Christians at Corinth:

> *"Examine yourselves, to see whether you are in the faith. Test yourselves. Or do you not realize*

this about yourselves, that Jesus Christ is in you?—unless indeed you fail to meet the test! (2 Cor. 13:5, ESV)."

Do we not know about ourselves that Jesus Christ is in us? How do we test ourselves? I assert that we can test it and know for certain by our courage to engage in this secret art of prayer as Jesus taught it, and try to disprove His method.

Test it and see for yourself. You cannot disprove it. What do you seek of Jesus? Examine your desire. Be honest without hidden motive. Go to Him in prayer. Ask of Him and feel that you have received your answer before you open your eyes. Trust in Him. Don't look back. Be faithful to the end.

You will receive, your joy will be made full, and you will find that He is, truly, within you.

11

The Method

For thirty-plus years I asked and asked and asked, and rarely received answers to my prayers. I emulated the words of good men who spoke beautiful prayers in worship, and in Bible studies, and in Bible classes.

I prayed to God who I believed to be afar off. I prayed through His Son who I believe to be afar off at God's right hand. I prayed morning, noon, and night with few results. I led prayers at worship services, at weddings, funerals, birthday parties, family reunions, and the like. I overhead some say, "Call on brother Shank – he leads a good prayer!" This means *he says good words and sounds like a seasoned Christian.* However, my results seemed somewhat pitiful at times.

Let's be honest. I went through the motions, attended all services, was active in ministry and preaching and teaching and counseling. I loved the Lord with all my heart and believed to the utmost extreme of my ability. I tried to bear fruits of the spirit, and fruits of my spiritual labors, and I tried to love all others– failing most of the time with that one, and did everything in my power to be the Christian example that my family could be proud of. But my prayer results were dismal.

And I've found through numerous private conversations with other Christians that my dismal results of prayer were the norm, and far more common than I had known.

I didn't know **how to pray**. I did not know that *"Hitherto have ye asked nothing in my name"* (John 16:24). I said words in prayer, and I closed every prayer with the words "In Jesus name I pray"; but *this* was not asking in His name.

Saying the words "in Jesus name" is not asking in His name.

I thought that I had asked in His name, but I did not know that the Lord had instructed to *"ask without hidden motive* (Aramaic texts which had been suppressed)".

Often times I would question and "judge" the "rightness" of my requests…

Is it okay for me to ask Him for a better job;

Am I asking for a better job so that I can provide my family with a better life – is that asking 'amiss' so that I can spend it on my own lusts;

Is it wrong to ask Him to heal my loved one;

Is it wrong to ask Him to bless me with money to buy new tires– my tires are bald and unsafe;

Is it evil to ask Him to help me with my addiction to nicotin– I chose to smoke that first cigarette, so I shouldn't expect help to stop.

My desires and requests came with an undue amount of motive and self-judgment.

I didn't know that in prayer I was to "*be surrounded by your answer* (Aramaic texts which had been suppressed).

I didn't know that in prayer I was to "*be enveloped by what you desire, that your gladness be full* (Aramaic texts which had been suppressed).

However, I remembered in times past when, during rare and specific prayers, I had somehow known that my prayer was already answered before finishing the prayer. I was in those rare times I was practicing being *surrounded* and *enveloped in what I desired,* but I didn't know what I was doing– yet, in spite of not knowing, *my gladness was made full.*

It was that *feeling* that I got.

Praying for a wife, praying for a computer job in Nashville, praying for the house to sell in 2019 so that we could move to the mountains… it was in those times when I got that *feeling*– regardless of how impossible the request seemed, my prayer was answered, and my gladness was made full.

It was in those rare occasions that I *"believed that I had received them* (Mark 11:24)" during and within those prayers.

In 2019 when I got that "feeling" and our house sold in a week– an impossibility, that I knew that there was something to that prayer event.

And I knew I was missing something.

In 2020 when I stumbled on Gregg Braden's video describing the missing Aramaic texts in John 16, it's as if the Lord connected the dots. I went back to Mark 11:24, and I began to study.

Over this past four years I have examined and tested myself over and over again by practicing prayer in the way described herein, and my results have been remarkable! I have found the Lord Jesus Christ within, and the joy that we have experienced is beyond words.

And yes, I've failed a lot; however, I've learned that my failures in prayer have always been when I did not pray until I got the "feeling", and doubt would set in. I would turn back after putting my hands to the plow, and unfit myself for the kingdom of God.

Brother and sister, this is Scripture. It is not new. It is not different. It is not unscriptural. I have, for four years, worked diligently at following the way that the Lord taught, and through many successes and failures, I bring this to you. It is completely up to you whether or not you want to test yourselves.

The method is simple. The scriptural principles must be maintained. You must remain faithful.

You must also engage the whole of your intellect, imagination, and mental focus. The art of prayer requires honest desire without motive, belief, acceptance, courage, an immersion (being surrounded, enveloped) into the belief and feeling that your prayer is answered during and within your prayer, and a child-like faith.

The method of effective prayer drawn exclusively from the Scriptures is as follows:

DESIRE. You Must Know What You Want.
And looking upon Jesus as he walked, he saith, Behold the Lamb of God! And the two disciples heard him speak, and they followed Jesus. Then Jesus turned, and saw them following, and saith unto them, "What seek ye?"

What seek ye? What are you looking for?
What do you want of Me?

We, like the two disciples hearing John point to the Savior, followed Jesus. We followed Him because we wanted something. We wanted salvation from our sins. We, all of us, wanted eternal life, and we wanted to escape Hell.

Did our needs and wants just disappear after coming out of the waters of baptism?

Life is filled with an array of problems and challenges that we want to overcome. What is it? Sickness, disease, poverty, a job loss, a broken relationship, a loss of meaning or purpose, loneliness… what seek ye?

The first step in successful prayer is to know what it is that you want. You know what it is without a second of thought.

BELIEF. Do You Believe That He is Willing and Able?

Jesus said to him, "If you can believe, all things are possible to him who believes. Immediately the father

Mark 9:23-24

Here is the unspoken question: Do you really believe? Not a philosophical or theological belief, but a believe that brings you to ask Him for what may seem as impossible?

Belief is the foundation of all successful prayer. Belief is the component which enables God to construct the bridge of incidence whereby He brings you to that outcome you so desire.

Ten thousand pages could be written on belief, and it wouldn't be enough. Belief, and your willingness and ability to believe, cannot be overemphasized. Our faith in Jesus Christ and His gospel begins in, and is enacted in, and is maintained in, and is grown in our core being– our inner man which we refer to as the "heart". It is more accurately our "mind".

Our mind is our garden where all seeds are planted and nurtured. It is within and through our minds that all life is created and springs forth into reality, for *as a man thinketh in his heart (mind), so is*

147

he (Prov. 23:7). Therefore, our future is created by our thoughts as seen in the words, *"so is he"*.

We witness an external negative thing; a fear or concern comes forth by our thoughts. The seed is planted in our garden. We think the worst. Our thinking, which is to water and nurture that seed, will produce a harvest.

This knowledge is powerful, because it means that we can weed the garden of negative and fearful thoughts. We can choose to plant a different seed which will produce the best possible outcome.

When we witness an external negative thing; a fear or concern comes forth by our thoughts. We remove the seed of negativity and the worst possible outcome by imaging the outcome we desire. We engage in prayer that our Father will intervene to change or modify things or events in our external world toward that which will give us relief, satisfaction– that our joy may be made full. In this way we tend to our garden and plant seeds that are good, and pure, and virtuous, and of good report, and we think on these things.

In example, we receive a text saying that our loved one was diagnosed with cancer (external event).

We immediately, without any effort, desire that our loved one is healed (a need comes forth from consciousness). We drop to our knees and pray, "Father, please heal my loved one" (intervene and change the current reality of sickness in my loved one). We desire relief from disease for our loved one, that their joy will be made full, and our joy will, thereby, be made full.

We must, within our prayer for our loved one, imagine within in innermost core that God hears us and wants to give to us that we might receive. This exercise of imagining that He has answered in the affirmative creates a *feeling within us*– a real, physical, palpable, emotional feeling that we have received at that moment what we ask Him for (be surrounded, enveloped, immersed in the answer), we will have it (Mark 11:24).

All of this requires belief; all is belief.

However, we're confronted with doubt…

What is wrong with you?

You seek a 'miracle'– don't you know the age of miracles has ceased?

Who gave you the authority to believe such a thing?

Go ahead and pray for a healing, but don't you dare tell others to think they can have such a thing– and don't tell them to pray for impossible outcomes!

Accept God's will and don't test Him with such requests!

You can't expect a healing– He doesn't do that today!

God works through doctors– if they can't cure it, then accept it and stop expecting such results.

The "hyper-religious" among us will sometimes find belief to be a most challenging aspect of the Christian faith. The Scribes and Pharisees hated Jesus for His statement that He and the Father were one. They hated Him for His works. When Jesus walked in the temple in Solomon's porch (John 10), he said to Jews round about Him, *"I and my Father are one."* Then the Jews took up stones again to stone him.

Jesus answered them, *"Many good works have I shewed you from my Father; for which of those works do ye stone me?"*

The Jews answered him, saying, *"For a good work we stone thee not; but for blasphemy; and because that thou, being a man, makest thyself God."*

Jesus answered them, *"Is it not written in your law, I said, Ye are gods? If he called them gods, unto whom the word of God came, and the scripture cannot be broken; Say ye of him, whom the Father hath sanctified, and sent into the world, Thou blasphemest; because I said, I am the Son of God? If I do not the works of my Father, believe me not. But if I do, though ye believe not me, believe the works: that ye may know, and believe, that the Father is in me, and I in him* (vv. 30-38)."

Those at that time who were highly educated in the Law and the Prophets found Jesus' claims to be "one with the Father" to be blasphemous. Jesus was revealing to them that the kingdom and the Father were in Him, and He boldly asserted pursuant to Psalm 82:6-7, *"Ye are gods"*, reminding them that the One true God of Abraham was within them, as well.

The same can be said of you. God is within you, as we are children of God by *the adoption by Jesus Christ to Himself, according to the good pleasure of His will* (Eph. 1:5); *for ye are all the*

*children of God by faith in Christ Jesus. For as many
of you as have been baptized into Christ have put on
Christ* (Gal. 3:26-27); *and if ye be Christ's, then are ye
Abraham's seed, and heirs according to the promise*
(v. 29).

Dear reader, *these things have I written unto
you that believe on the name of the Son of God* (1 Jo.
5:13); *And this is the confidence that we have in him,
that, if we ask any thing according to his will, he
heareth us: And if we know that he hear us, whatsoever
we ask, we know that we have the petitions that we
desired of him* (vv. 14-15).

Will you believe?

Belief is the critical element. Belief is required
without negotiation. Belief is the bold and courageous
willingness to imagine, and remain faithful to, our
desired outcome, *because greater is he that is in you,
than he that is in the world* (1 Jo. 4:4).

I believe; help thou mine unbelief (Mark 9:24)

GO INTO THY CLOSET. Closing Off the Senses:
*But thou, when thou prayest, enter into thy closet, and
when thou hast shut thy door, pray to thy Father which*

Matthew 6:6

I have engaged in hundreds of prayer experiments since February of 2019, spurred by the seeming impossible answer to my prayer for the sale of our home, and our move to the mountains.

That prayer and answer that followed enlightened me with the knowledge that the answer was somehow connected to my "feeling of having received the answer within the prayer", as stated by Jesus in Mark 11:24.

I have found, through these hundreds of experiments and combined with a careful study of the scriptures, specific methods which help me to enter into the feeling of the answered prayer.

Effective prayer is done in a state akin to sleep. This state is simply allowing yourself to relax completely.

Our brains constantly produce bursts of electrical pulses, or waves. Each wave operates at a different speed. These speeds are categorized as gamma, beta, alpha, theta, and delta. A test called an electroencephalogram (EEG) can evaluate the electrical activity in your brain and record the waves, which are measured in cycles per second, or Hertz (Hz). Gamma waves are the fastest; delta waves are the slowest.

As we relax, our brain waves slow. We move from gamma down to theta. At theta we fall into sleep. It is said that delta waves are produced in deep sleep. Our goal is to still ourselves and relax so that we can slow the brain and move into the alpha state, which is the state just before sleep. It is the state akin, or closest to, sleep.

The command for prayer is to go into your closet, shut the door behind you, and pray to the Father in secret (Matt. 6:6). This is not literal in the gross first sense; this instruction is telling man to find a quiet place that is free from external noise and distractions, and to shut off all senses (sight, hearing, feeling, taste, touch). We are to *be still, and know that I am God* (Psalm 46:10).

We must find a place of seclusion that is free from external influences, and close our eyes. As we rest in darkness and focus on the kingdom within, our senses of hearing, and smell, and taste, and touch will begin to diminish. Our breathing will slow, and we will fall into complete relaxation.

We must not fall into sleep, but we must move close to it. Once reached, we know that we have entered into our closet and shut the door behind us (Matt. 6:6).

There, in that state, we begin to contemplate our desire, thus bringing it before the Lord and with the knowledge that He is hearing us; *and if we know that he hear us, whatsoever we ask, we know that we have the petitions that we desired of him* (1 Jo. 5:15).

We present our petitions to the Lord without hidden motive– without judgment that our request is right or wrong or good or bad, for He already knows our heart.

As we make our petitions known to Him, we begin to imagine that He has, at that moment and in that space, answered our request in the affirmative. Begin to imagine and visualize already having what you are asking for. Create a scene in your mind that would be if your prayer was answered, then imagine the feeling… what would it feel like to have your answer? Relief? Satisfaction? Rejoicing? How do others act and respond by the affirmative answer? Can you hear their words of appreciation, gratitude, and celebration?

As you contemplate and feel your answer, you will be surrounded and enveloped by the feelings of love, relief, satisfaction, gratitude, and great rejoicing. You will, at this moment, be immersed in the result–baptized in the answer. You will arise from your prayer with great rejoicing.

Begin to express your gratitude to the Lord before you end your prayer, as it is by this that you *enter into his gates with thanksgiving, and into his courts with praise: be thankful unto him, and bless his name* (Psalm 100:4).

You have, through these methods and steps, asked in His name, and you shall receive, that your joy may be full (Jo. 16:23-24). Search the scriptures and see for yourself whether these things be so.

Why is the feeling such a critical component? Jesus said, *"Therefore I say unto you, What things soever ye desire, when ye pray, **believe that ye receive them**, and ye shall have them* (Mark 11:24)". It's with a measure of difficulty that man believes that he's received something that he does not yet see or have; therefore, the command to believe that you receive before you receive is a challenge in successful prayer, but **it must be accomplished** if we are to have the answers to our prayers.

To achieve this belief, we must imagine and visualize that we have our answer. Our imagining should, if believed, produce a palpable, physical, emotional *feeling* with us– you can't stop it or prevent it, because it is a natural physiological and emotional response.

When we pray in this way and the feeling is produced, we metaphorically *touch the hem of His garment and virtue goes out of Him*:

> *"And a woman having an issue of blood twelve years, which had spent all her living upon physicians, neither could be healed of any, Came behind him, and touched the border of his garment: and immediately her issue of blood stanched. And Jesus said, Who touched me? When all denied, Peter and they that were with him said, Master, the multitude throng thee and press thee, and sayest thou, Who touched me? And Jesus said, Somebody hath touched me: for I perceive that virtue is gone out of me. And when the woman saw that she*

*was not hid, she came trembling, and falling
down before him, she declared unto him before
all the people for what cause she had touched
him, and how she was healed immediately.
And he said unto her, Daughter, be of good
comfort: thy faith hath made thee whole; go in
peace.*" Luke 8:43-48

It is this faith– this *feeling* that we receive what
we ask for before we receive it that is the metaphorical
touching of His hem. (Lk. 8:46).

This would be perfect place to remind you of
what Gregg Braden referred to in his discussion of the
lost (suppressed) Aramaic texts, "When you make the
two, thought and emotion, become one– when you
make the two 'one' [within your mind and heart], you
will say to the mountain, 'Move away,' and the
mountain will move away… when thought and
emotion become one, the feeling [power] is created in
our body."

This method of prayer to our Lord provides to
us the methodology for *asking in His name*, as it is the
marrying of our thoughts and emotions into one flesh,

thus enabling virtue to go out from our Lord within each one of us.

There is a fascinating story in the New Testament of ten men that were lepers who confronted Jesus:

"And it came to pass, as he went to Jerusalem, that he passed through the midst of Samaria and Galilee. And as he entered into a certain village, there met him ten men that were lepers, which stood afar off: And they lifted up their voices, and said, Jesus, Master, have mercy on us. And when he saw them, he said unto them, Go shew yourselves unto the priests. And it came to pass, that, as they went, they were cleansed.

And one of them, when he saw that he was healed, turned back, and with a loud voice glorified God, And fell down on his face at his feet, giving him thanks: and he was a Samaritan. And Jesus answering said, Were there not ten cleansed? But where are the nine?

There are not found that returned to give glory to God, save this stranger. And he said unto him, Arise, go thy way: thy faith hath made thee whole." Luke 17:11-19

The elements are remarkable when identified and considered. Ten lepers. Ten is representative of the 10th letter of the Hebrew alphabet: Yod, " ‫י‬ " (also spelled Yud).
It is the first letter of the hidden name of God: YHWH. The letter "Yod" in God's name means "Hand", which is God's power, the Hand that creates and fashions. It is represented in the English alphabet as the letter "J".

The ten confront Jesus and did *not* make the explicit request for healing, but rather exclaimed that He have mercy on them.

Jesus did not command them to be healed, nor did He state that they were healed, but rather, *"Go shew yourselves unto the priests."*

No performance of a miracle, no command of healing, and no implication that He healed them on the spot.

As a matter of contextual fact, notice *when* they were healed (cleansed): "*And it came to pass, that,* ***as they went, they were cleansed.***"

This is significant because it demonstrates components of biblical faith not expressed in the text:

- Jesus told the lepers to go to the high-ranking religious official to show him; show him what, exactly? They were not yet healed; they were still lepers.

- The command to go implied healing by their arrival.

- The command also implies that the lepers were to believe that they had their desire (healing) before they could see the evidence.

- This connects to Mark 11:24, "*believe that ye receive them* (before you see results that you have them), *and ye shall have them.*"

- The lepers would, in order to show true faith in Jesus, be required to obey Him, thereby acting without hesitation to go and show.

We must know that when these men looked at their own skin and saw no change, they were then confronted with the dilemma, *"Am I to go and show the priest my diseased skin?"*

To go without proof and evidence required immense faith in the words of Jesus Christ.

To go without proof and evidence would demonstrate the faith spoken of in Hebrews 11.

To go without proof and evidence would require remarkable courage on the part of the lepers.

Their acceptance and subsequent obedience demonstrated a sacrificial faith– the type of faith shown by Abraham when he took the knife to slay his son.

Notice the shock as one of them saw during their journey that he was healed, as it is written, *"And one of them, when he saw that he was healed, turned back, and with a loud voice glorified God, And fell down on his face at his feet, giving him thanks: and he was a Samaritan.* " It is in that *feeling*– that shock and awe and uncontrollable gratitude to God that follows which is what we seek in prayer.

At what moment and by what element were the lepers healed? We see it in the close of the story: *And he said unto him, Arise, go thy way: thy faith hath made thee whole.*"

The moment was when they trusted Him enough to hear and accept His words to "go and show yourself to the priest". Their movement toward the priest was their act of faith, and it was their faith that made them whole.

Dear reader, it is your faith that will make you whole. It is your belief that you already have what you ask of Him, and your feeling generated from the marrying of your thought and emotion that will enable the Lord to do for you what you ask of Him.

Will you believe, accept, and obey this command of Christ when you are confronted with such need?

This concept of faith isn't taught in the churches today. To pray and believe you already have what you ask in order to receive what you ask is in accord with Mark 11:24 as taught by Jesus and is received and obeyed by His followers, but it is not taught or known today by any that I've met in Christendom. This is one of the hidden secrets of the art of prayer. It is one element of which those throughout history have scoffed at the way.

12
Bridge of Incident

Incident means an event, an occurrence, or a moment that may or may not be expected. I refer to as "the unfolding".

It is written, "*And we know that all things work together for good to them that love God, to them who are the called according to his purpose*" (Rom. 8:28). I believe that this verse has been so overused that it has lost impact in what is implied under the surface.

When you and I pray *in His name*, which was explained in the previous chapter, the Lord creates at the moment of our *feeling that we have received*, a bridge constructed of incidents that will unfold in the coming hours and days– IF we tend the garden.

The incidents will unfold before us as we walk in the light and hold confidently to the outcome that we have thanked Him for.

You walk, after successful prayer, across a bridge of incidents that may, on the surface, seem irrelevant and unconnected. It unfolds via the power of your assumptive belief– *I have* [present tense] *what I asked Him for, and I thank Him continually.*

You must live from this position of having received your answer already, so that you may receive your answer in the near future. Remember His words, *"believe that ye receive them, and **ye shall have them*** (Mark 11:24)." You must remember that receiving them [future tense] is completely dependent upon your confident, absolute belief that you already received them [past tense]. This is *the way*. His way. The New Testament is replete with proof via narrative example (i.e., The Ten Lepers).

In this way you live in the end– you live in and from the vantage point that you already have what you asked for. This "lifestyle" opposes reason and logic. It creates internal conflict for men who demand a working plan of action before committing to an idea. Living in the end seems foolish to those who do not practice faith in the extreme.

Living in the end is the daily application and practical demonstration of what we claim in such a "tongue-in-cheek" manner– *for we walk by faith, not by sight* (2 Cor. 5:7). Many who profess Christ find great satisfaction in making the claim of walking by faith, but to pray in the way I've revealed herein and to live in the end with absolute confidence that we have what we asked for– what we call assumptive belief, requires you to muster a courage not before seen.

Living in the end is accomplished by the constant meditation upon the facts of why faith is required, and what faith means: 1) We know that He is a reward of them that diligently seek Him; 2) we know that without faith we cannot please Him; 3) we understand that faith is the very substance of the things we hope for; and 4) faith is the evidence of what is not seen.

These principles must be repeated until they become part of our personality. Our thinking must be steeped in these ideas and concepts to a point whereby our belief and confidence is that of a child– child-like faith.

In July of 2019 we received into our custody our grandson, Corban, who was eight months old at the time. We became his full-time mother/father, and we did and still do raise him as our very own.

Shortly after he began walking, Corban enjoyed getting into our king-sized bed with us for a few minutes before putting him into his own bed. After a few minutes and announcing to him that it was time for him to be put into his bed, he would stand up on the king-bed and want to run and jump off of our bed into my arms. This was great fun, and it became part of our nightly routine.

When Corban was around twenty months old, he was in our king-bed with Jonetta, and I was seated in a recliner on the other side of the bed.

Jonetta checked the clock and said, "Corban, it's your bedtime", which signaled for him to get up.

At that moment I realized what was about to happen. Looking up from my recliner I saw Corban stand up…

Dear God, he's going to do it!

Corban was starting his run toward the edge of the bed. Our king-bed sits very high– we have to "climb" up to get into it.

I was seated on the other side of the bed opposite of Corban, and on the other side of the edge he was going to leap from. Jonetta was in bed and in no position to help.

I jumped up and tried to get to him– Jonetta screamed!

I barely made it to him. Corban jumped off the bed without ever looking at me or looking in my direction. He ran and jumped into the air off of the side of that tall bed without me being there to catch him.

And I'm not exaggerating when I tell you that I just barely made it– I caught him *in the air* after having scrambled out of the chair and racing to his projected position.

Corban thought it was great fun! We, however, did not.

I realized that Corban had, night after night, developed a deep and unquestionable faith that I would catch him. He knew without a shred of doubt that his paw-paw would never let him hit the floor.

He knew I would not fail him.

Corban knew when he ran to the edge of the bed that I would not– I could not let him down.

Be strong and of a good courage, fear not, nor be afraid of them: for the Lord thy God, he it is that doth go with thee; he will not fail thee, nor forsake thee (Deut. 31:6).

And the Lord, he it is that doth go before thee; he will be with thee, he will not fail thee, neither forsake thee: fear not, neither be dismayed (Deut. 31:8).

My failures in prayer and my perception that the Lord had abandoned me were a direct result of me asking amiss– I had asked wrongly.

No, I had not asked Him for a wrong *thing*.

I'd asked in the wrong *way*.

I'd never asked *in His name*.

Why? Because I didn't know how.

I had spent years closing every prayer with the words, "In Jesus name I pray", but saying those words was not, as we now know, asking in His name.

We have, through the discovery of previously suppressed texts, and a deeper scriptural study, and hundreds of experiments in prayer, found what it means to "ask in His name".

When you and I approach Jesus Christ within, and we go into the closet and close off the senses, and when we make our petitions known unto Him, and when we visualize, imagine, and *feel the feeling* of how it would feel to have received our answer, and when we know that we have our answer at the moment which brings us into involuntary rejoicing and gratitude before we come out of that prayer, **we have asked in His name**. We have done as He has commanded. We've obeyed the Lord.

We must then, after successfully asking in His name, walk the bridge of incidents in faith that He makes our paths straight (Prov. 3:6). It will be to that end that we will bear witness to the answer to our prayer.

It is in *this way* that He *works all things together for good to them that love God, to them who are the called according to his purpose.*

I've always closed my prayers with, "In Jesus' name I pray", but now I understand what it means to ask in His name.

13

The Unfitting of Self

"A man's mind may be likened to a garden, which may

be intelligently cultivated or allowed to run wild; but

whether cultivated or neglected, it must, and will, bring

forth. If no useful seeds are put into it, then an

abundance of useless weed seeds will fall therein, and

will continue to produce their kind."

–James Allen, As a Man Thinketh

Every aspect of our faith happens first in our mind– the garden. It is, therefore, crucial to understand that our most important asset is our mind, and our most important task is to guard and tend to our garden.

Thoughts are seeds. These seeds may be planted deeply by feeling and emotions. The seeds are watered and nurtured by the frequency that we return to the seed-bed, and by our attention and focus that we pay to its cultivation– our attention as likened to the sun. It is the sun which provides the energy and power necessary for the seed to grow. We water the seed with our feelings and emotions. Planting a seed into our garden, whether it be good seed or bad, and continuing to give it sunlight and water will cause it to sprout. If we focus on that seed as an important and singular plant, and thereby removing all other seeds around it, the plant will grow quickly and will produce a harvest.

Our conscious effort to remove our attention and focus away from a seed, even one previously planted, will cause the seed to die.

To continually check the seed is to dig it up– to disturb it, and such checking will impede the seed or even kill it.

There is a biblical story which gives insight into these concepts. It is the story of Daniel:

It pleased Darius to set over the kingdom an hundred and twenty princes, which should be over the whole kingdom;

And over these three presidents; of whom Daniel was first: that the princes might give accounts unto them, and the king should have no damage.

Then this Daniel was preferred above the presidents and princes, because an excellent spirit was in him; and the king thought to set him over the whole realm.

Then the presidents and princes sought to find occasion against Daniel concerning the kingdom; but they could find none occasion nor fault; forasmuch as he was faithful, neither was there any error or fault found in him.

Then said these men, We shall not find any occasion against this Daniel, except we find it against him concerning the law of his God.

Then these presidents and princes assembled together to the king, and said thus unto him, King Darius, live for ever.

All the presidents of the kingdom, the governors, and the princes, the counsellors, and the captains, have consulted together to establish a royal statute, and to make a firm decree, that whosoever shall ask a petition of any God or man for thirty days, save of thee, O king, he shall be cast into the den of lions.

Now, O king, establish the decree, and sign the writing, that it be not changed, according to the law of the Medes and Persians, which altereth not.

Wherefore king Darius signed the writing and the decree.

Now when Daniel knew that the writing was signed, he went into his house; and his windows being open in his chamber toward Jerusalem, he kneeled upon his knees three times a day, and prayed, and gave thanks before his God, as he did aforetime.

Then these men assembled, and found Daniel praying and making supplication before his God.

Then they came near, and spake before the king concerning the king's decree; Hast thou not signed a decree, that every man that shall ask a petition of any God or man within thirty days, save of thee, O king, shall be cast into the den of lions? The king answered and said, The thing is true, according to the law of the Medes and Persians, which altereth not.

Then answered they and said before the king, That Daniel, which is of the children of the captivity of Judah, regardeth not thee, O king, nor the decree that thou hast signed, but maketh his petition three times a day.

Then the king, when he heard these words, was sore displeased with himself, and set his heart on Daniel to deliver him: and he laboured till the going down of the sun to deliver him.

Then these men assembled unto the king, and said unto the king, Know, O king, that the law of the Medes and Persians is, That no decree nor statute which the king establisheth may be changed.

Then the king commanded, and they brought Daniel, and cast him into the den of lions. Now the king spake and said unto Daniel, Thy God whom thou servest continually, he will deliver thee.

And a stone was brought, and laid upon the mouth of the den; and the king sealed it with his own signet, and with the signet of his lords; that the purpose might not be changed concerning Daniel.

Then the king went to his palace, and passed the night fasting: neither were instruments of musick brought before him: and his sleep went from him.

Then the king arose very early in the morning, and went in haste unto the den of lions.

And when he came to the den, he cried with a lamentable voice unto Daniel: and the king spake and said to Daniel, O Daniel, servant of the living God, is thy God, whom thou servest continually, able to deliver thee from the lions?

Then said Daniel unto the king, O king, live for ever.

My God hath sent his angel, and hath shut the lions' mouths, that they have not hurt me: forasmuch as before him innocency was found in me; and also before thee, O king, have I done no hurt.

Then was the king exceedingly glad for him, and commanded that they should take Daniel up out of the den. So Daniel was taken up out of the den, and no manner of hurt was found upon him, because he believed in his God.

And the king commanded, and they brought those men which had accused Daniel,

*and they cast them into the den of lions, them,
their children, and their wives; and the lions
had the mastery of them, and brake all their
bones in pieces or ever they came at the bottom
of the den.*

*Then king Darius wrote unto all people,
nations, and languages, that dwell in all the
earth; Peace be multiplied unto you.*

*I make a decree, That in every dominion
of my kingdom men tremble and fear before the
God of Daniel: for he is the living God, and
stedfast for ever, and his kingdom that which
shall not be destroyed, and his dominion shall
be even unto the end.*

*He delivereth and rescueth, and he
worketh signs and wonders in heaven and in
earth, who hath delivered Daniel from the
power of the lions.*

*So this Daniel prospered in the reign of
Darius, and in the reign of Cyrus the Persian.*

Daniel 6:1-28, KJV

The end of this story reveals that Daniel
prevailed and prospered. The story gives us a

powerful phycological insight into several aspects of the concepts set forth in this book.

We, like Daniel are followers of the Lord. We have the spirit of the Lord within (Luke 17:21). The earthly King Darius set 120 princes over the kingdom, and over these were 3 presidents– Daniel was one of the 3 presidents, and he was preferred over all because of the excellent spirit within him (v. 3). This caused the others to resent Daniel to the point of seeking to find a way to accuse and unseat him (vv. 4-5).

The royals and presidents and cabinet then devised a plan to enact a law that outlawed prayer to any god or any man other than to King Darius, that any such person would be executed via consumption by lions (vv. 6-9).

Daniel disregarded the law and continued to pray to Jehovah God three times each day, as he had always done (v. 10).

He was arrested, brought before the king, and cast into the den for execution (vv. 11-17). That night the king, who loved Daniel, fasted and went without sleep (v. 18).

The next morning the king and his cabinet found Daniel alive. Daniel glorified and credited God who sent His angel to close the mouths of the lions (vv. 19-23).

We, like Daniel, face problems that appear to be bringing us to our demise. There seems to be no way out, and when we're cast into a pit of destruction whereby, we come face to face with apparent death, we must know what to do.

Daniel, upon being cast into a den of lions who would devour him and take his life, looked away. Daniel turned his back to the lions, and he looked to the Light – he turned his focus and attention toward God. To turn away from our problems is to be renewed and transformed in the spirit of our mind.

This is what we must do. In the face of every problem, we must turn away. We must find the courage and the strength to remove our focus (i.e., our mental attention, our meditation on the problem, our anxiety and worry and fears, our emotions and feelings), and we must turn all attention toward God, the Source of our power within.

It is only in this way that our God will save us. If we pick up a rock and attempt to fight the lions, we're giving into our fears, and we're removing the problem from God's capable hands in our attempt to fight by our own wisdom and power.

"Be still, and know that I am God: I will be exalted among the heathen, I will be exalted in the earth (Psalm 46:10)." We are to be still in the face of certain destruction.

"Humble yourselves therefore under the mighty hand of God, that he may exalt you in due time: Casting all your care upon him; for he careth for you. Be sober, be vigilant; because your adversary the devil, as a roaring lion, walketh about, seeking whom he may devour (1 Pet. 5:6-8)."

We are all prey hunted by a lion who walks about seeking to destroy us (*Ibid*). The practical advice is to humble ourselves, and to cast our every care upon Him (*Ibid*). We speak of this "casting of our cares", but it is within and through our prayers that we execute the command.

I have learned that I pray as discussed herein, I've experienced that *peace of God which passeth all understanding* (Phil. 4:7).

When we arise from prayer with the knowing that we have already received our answer, and we begin to walk the bridge of incidents leading to our outcome, we must remain faithful to that end.

The first challenge is to know how to pray. The second is to pray successfully, generating and experiencing the feeling of the answered prayer. The third challenge is to remain faithful to the end.

I have, personally, found this to be the most difficult and challenging part of prayer.

Let's consider a practical example:

You have lost your job to no fault of your own. You have only a few hundred dollars left in your checking account due to previous circumstances that exhausted your savings.

You have no resources, no savings, no family to borrow from. You have children to provide for, and your wife cannot work outside the home because child-care would cost more than her potential salary.

Your rent is due in three weeks. It's $1,500.00. You have no income, no resources, and around $250.00 left in your account.

What do you want?

Jesus asks from within, *"What do you want of Me?"*

Income. A job so that I may provide for my family. And immediate money to my bills and upcoming rent.

You determine a need for a realistic amount of $3,500.00. Your desire is a job and $3,500.00.

You know what you want. You know what you must have.

You now go to the Lord in prayer and *ask in His name*: you, within prayer, generate a scene using your imagining faculty (imagination) where you have received $3,500.00 and a new job.

You imagine yourself calling your wife and telling her of this wonderful answer to prayer. You hear her voice thanking God over and over. You feel how it would feel to have your answer. You experience the relief and satisfaction that would be yours if you had these things that you ask of Him. You begin thanking Him within with such joy and gratitude as you accept the idea that you now have what you asked for.

You arise from the prayer rejoicing within a peace that goes beyond anything that you've ever felt in the past – a peace that goes beyond understanding, and you fear not, because all of your cares have now been cast upon Him, for He careth for you.

The following morning you are having breakfast and your phone rings. It's your bank informing you that your automatic-payment for your cell-phone bill was deducted from your account by your cellular provider, and your account is now overdrawn by $200.00. You, in the previous stress of the loss of your job, forgot about the auto-payment.

The feeling of the answered prayer disappears. Your previous confidence and relaxed state of being is destroyed, as you are now in the lion's den.

Panic overwhelms you.

All is lost! How could God leave me in such a place after I placed my trust and faith into Him and His care? I was so sure He had answered my prayer— it's a promise He made, and I asked in Jesus' name! I was so sure He would provide for me and my family!

"*Lord,*" you return to Him in prayer after calming yourself. You're in closet and you've shut the door behind you.

"*I cannot believe You've allowed this after I was so sure that I had what I asked You for. I am in the lion's den, but I refuse to take my hands from the plow. I'll not look back at Sodom. I will look forward. Help me, dear Lord, to take my attention away from these problems that are at my back and ready to devour me. Give me the strength to hold to my faith in the Lord Jesus Christ and His power to save. I have planted the seed. I was surrounded in my answer. I was enveloped in the feeling that He gave to me what I asked Him for."*

Your phone rings again interrupting your prayer. The bank asks you to come to the branch to discuss your account. For some reason they need you to come now. Your stomach is in a knot.

Upon arriving at the bank you're escorted to a conference room. The banker opens her laptop and accesses the bank's records.

"We apologize. It appears as though a deposit was made into your account a few minutes ago," she says in a puzzled tone.

"What?" you reply.

"Yes, I see it here. It came from your employer– the memo says, "Final deposit from retirement program."

"I didn't know I had a retirement plan with them," you say softly. Dumbfounded. "How much was the deposit?" you manage to ask.

"$8,300.00," says the banker.

You leave the room and walk toward the door through the lobby. You're in a daze… someone calls your name. You look– it's an old friend.

"Hey, it's weird seeing you here! I was just thinking about you this morning. You're not looking for a job, are you?" asks your old friend.

"A job?" *A job!* "Yeah, yeah, as a matter of fact, I *am* looking for a job!"

"Great! We had to let a guy go last night. Got a late call saying he'd gotten a DUI. It's weird, but I thought of you last night after the call. You'd be a perfect fit for the role that's open. Listen, text me tonight and we'll get you in for an interview tomorrow morning– if you'll show up, the job is yours!"

You're completely shocked. Adrenaline is coursing through your veins as you're beginning to realize all that has happened.

You are experiencing the feeling– the identical feeling that you experienced within your prayer.

You've *felt* this feeling– you *felt it* during your prayer– the *feeling of your answered prayer.*

Assumptive belief.

Go thy way; your faith has made you whole.

"8,300.00. We're ok. We're going to make it through. That was more than I asked. And a job! A new job! He did it all! He answered my prayers! He really answered my prayers!"

You're reminded of Ephesians: *"Now unto him that is able to do exceeding abundantly above all that we ask or think, according to the power that worketh in us (3:20)."*

Assumptive belief.

The Lord created a bridge of incidents.

It appeared as though destruction was upon you, but He had already made His plan for you by your assumptive belief that generated the feeling within your prayer that your desire was fulfilled. You remained faithful in spite of being cast into the lion's den, and God didn't forsake you. He didn't fail you. Your faith made you whole.

So many will inadvertently unfit themselves for the kingdom. They will, after successful prayer, give into thoughts of fear and doubt. This is taking your hands from the plow and looking back. Jesus said, *"And Jesus said unto him, No man, having put his hand to the plough, and looking back, is fit for the kingdom of God* (Luke 9:62).

The kingdom of God is within baptized believers (Luke 17:21). When you, as a child of God, are confronted with a life-challenge, you are equally provided a solution via the power of Jesus Christ within you.

You can accept His promise of salvation of your problem through *asking in His name*, and remaining faithful until you see the death of your problem through the delivery of His answer to your prayer. This act is "putting your hands to the plow".

If you return to your problem by falling into fear and doubt, and if you are constantly checking to see if He has answered, you are taking your hands from the plow and looking back– unfitting yourself for the kingdom, and you become as a pillar of salt, preserved in that state.

It is written, *"But his wife looked back from behind him, and she became a pillar of salt* (Genesis 19:26). The hidden meaning of the Genesis story is that we are not to look back at our former life, lest we are preserved (turned to salt) in that state. Looking back is likened to taking our hands from the plow. We must follow the instructions given to Lot, *"Escape for thy life; look not behind thee* (Genesis 19:17). You do not look back.

Instead remember, there is *but this one thing I do, forgetting those things which are behind, and reaching forth unto those things which are before, I press toward the mark for the prize of the high calling of God in Christ Jesus* (Eph. 3:13-14).

Looking back is to unfit yourself for the kingdom. Hold fast to your desired outcome in faith with complete confidence in Jesus Christ, as the lepers journeying toward the Priest, and you will be cleansed along the way, for He *is able to do exceeding abundantly above all that we ask or think, according to the power that worketh in us* (Eph. 3:20).

Every aspect of your faith *first* happens in your mind– the garden. It is, therefore, crucial to understand that your most important asset is our mind, and your most important task is to guard and tend to your garden.

It is within these times that you and I are called to be mindful, and ever present, so that we do not risk unfitting ourselves for the kingdom.

Remember that it was in that moment when the bank called and you found that you were overdrawn, and all hope was lost, that you were to count it as joy (James 1).

As unrealistic and impractical as it sounds, trials are when we apply the advice, *"My brethren, count it all joy when ye fall into divers temptations; Knowing this, that the trying of your faith worketh patience (James 1:2-3)."*

When we're faced with such devastation, and it appears as though all hope is lost, and we fall into the temptation to yield to the loss, and reject our faith in the Lord, we must remember that the trying of our faith is working patience. Patience, if applied, will complete its perfect work, that you'll be perfect and complete in the Lord, leaving you wanting nothing (James 1:4).

Prepare now so that you may not unfit yourself for the kingdom.

<u>14</u>

I Am Your Potter

In April of 2023, I had a profound experience on a Colorado trail. While I hesitate to share the experience publicly, you need to hear it…

We received word on March 31, 2023, that a business event occurred which would devastate our book ministry. It was out of our control. I perceived that God had failed me because of the event, as the degree of devastation and the subsequent struggle to repair the damage that would ensue in the coming months and years to follow would be too much to overcome.

I had prayed fervently, and in spite of my best efforts, the event happened in direct opposition to my most heartfelt prayers and expectations of salvation from the problem.

I had not, at that point, fully understood the concepts outlined in this book. Furthermore, I can see (in hindsight) that the Lord was using the event to guide me onto a more specific path that would not have been realized had it not been for this devastating occurrence.

We are still, as of this writing, trying to recover. We're slowly and painful fulfilling all of the back-ordered books from that time, and we will fulfill all of them with the Lord's gracious help and blessing. We've been so grateful to the many Christians who have demonstrated their love, patience, and understanding through this time.

It was quickly after the occurrence of this horrible event that the following experience– something very shocking and profound, unfolded before me. I need you to understand how resistant I am to share this with you, because when it happened it was, at first, completely bizarre, and unorthodox– even a little woo-woo! I am not one who goes in for such things, but it happened. I now believe I know why.

On March 31, 2023, our faith was damaged to a severity that I had not previously believed was possible. Throughout that day I prayed, and I finally began to get a grasp of the pressure that is described in Christ's grief and anxiety expressed while He was in the garden.

"Count it all joy when ye fall into divers temptations (James 1:2, KJV)." The CEB translates it, *"Think of the various tests you encounter as occasions for joy."* I'd quoted this verse to discouraged brethren a hundred times before, but I couldn't, at that moment,

do it myself. There was no joy in what had happened, and I didn't have the mental strength to transform it into an occasion for joy.

Where are you, God?

How could You have let this happen?

You haven't kept your promises to me!

I am so angry with You!

What good is this faith?

Where is Jesus if He is in me as You say?

The hope of Jesus in me is gone. My hope is gone.

I cannot overemphasize that my faith was, at that moment– in spite of the decades spent following Christ, and the years spent in ministry, and the books published and distributed, and the many successes– collapsing.

I had spent months asking the Father, *"Where is the Son? What does Paul mean by the mystery of Christ within u – the hope of glory? If Jesus is not in a far off realm, but instead within me, show me!"*

I'd studied Paul's words in Ephesians 3:4, *"How that by revelation he made known unto me the mystery; (as I wrote afore in few words, whereby, when ye read, ye may understand my knowledge in the mystery of Christ).*" What was this "mystery of Christ"?

I had spent hours in search of what Paul meant by his statement in Colossians 1:27, "*To whom God would make known what is the riches of the glory of this mystery among the Gentiles; which is Christ in you, the hope of glory.*" I am a Gentile– what is this mystery among the Gentiles? Is Christ not in me? Do I not have this hope of glory?

I was again brought back to that one verse that seemed to eat at my mind… Ephesians 3:20:

> *Now unto him that is able to do exceeding abundantly above all that we ask or think, according to the power that worketh in us,* (ASV).

> *Now unto him that is able to do exceeding abundantly above all that we ask or think, according to the power that worketh in us,* (KJV).

> *Glory to God, who is able to do far beyond all that we could ask or imagine by his power at work within us,* (CEV).

Isn't Jesus Christ the power that's works within us?

If He IS in us, where is He in us?

How could He be in us?

He's not in my stomach! He's not in the organ that pumps my blood– the 'heart' is a reference to my inner-most being, isn't it?

Where is He?

How does He work?

How can I have been a Christian this long and not know the answers to these things?

Why won't God SHOW ME THIS MYSTERY?

We got into bed at 9:00 that evening. Jonetta read as she always does. I lied on my back and struggled to get control of my mind.

Relax. Breathe.

Breathe deep.

A thought came into my mind as though someone else was speaking. It was so "loud" and so seemingly "audible" that it startled me–

I Am your Potter.

I quickly sat up in bed.

"What's wrong!" asked Jonetta.

"Nothing," I responded. "Nothing, I just need to look at something.

"Where are you going?" she interrupted.

"I need my Bible," I responded. I was, in reality, thinking, "*You're loosing it! You're loosing your mind!*"

The verse was Jeremiah 18:2-4:

Arise, and go down to the potter's house, and there I will cause thee to hear my words. Then I went down to the potter's house, and, behold, he wrought a work on the wheels. And the vessel that he made of clay was marred in the hand of the potter: so he made it again another vessel, as seemed good to the potter to make it.

I again considered the thought, "*I Am your Potter*," and looked further. In Zachariah 11:12-13 we find:

Then I said to them, 'If it seems good to you, give me my wages; but if not, keep them.' And they weighed out as my wages thirty pieces of silver. Then the Lord said to me, "Throw it to the potter"– the lordly price at which I was priced by them. So I took the thirty pieces of silver and threw them into the house of the Lord, to the potter (ESV).

What did this mean? How is He the Potter?

Jeremiah 18:2-4 uses the Hebrew word "hay·yō·w·ṣêr"; Strong's 3335[e] "Yatsar", meaning "to form as in to create, or to fashion". It's the same word used in Zachariah.

Into the house of the Lord, to the Potter (Zach. 11:13). *I Am your Potter. Man is the temple of God, the Potter* (1 Cor. 3:16-17). *The Potter– the One Who Forms, is in His house, the temple, the kingdom– the kingdom is without you* (Luke 17:21). *I and the Potter are, therefore, one. Now go down to the Potter's house and I will see Him working at His wheel* (Jer. 18:2-4).

The text draws a singular conclusion. The Father and His Son reside within us, the Christian, in His house– His temple, which we're told by Paul (by inspiration of the Holy Spirit) is man.

It is revealed that He is the One that forms; therefore, He, our "Former" and "Fashioner", must reside within our thinking faculty– our mind. If this is the case, what is our creative faculty? It is our gift of creating and forming– it's that thing that we refer to as our "imagining faculty". The imagination.

Does the Jehovah God, the God of the Old Testament who made Himself manifest in and through His Son, Jesus Christ reside within the Christian's mind? Does He form and fashion and guide our life through the power of our mind, and through that creative faculty we casually refer to as our "imagining" function?

Blasphemy. What a blasphemous thought. What an absolutely ridiculous thought. My Father and His Son does, I agree, reside within the Christian. I couldn't figure out where or how, but I believed the scriptures– they were somehow "within".

I Am your Potter.

It was almost 11:00, and Jonetta was asleep. Her book on her chest. I gently removed it book and pulled the covers up to her chin.

This horrible day is almost over.

I got back into bed and closed my eyes.

I Am your Potter.

It wouldn't stop.

I Am your Potter.

Yes, it was confirmed. I *was* losing my mind.

I Am your Potter, Jeremiah 18. I Am your mind– the mind of Christ, 1 Corinthians 2. Examine yourselves, whether ye be in the faith; prove your own selves. Know ye not your own selves, how that Jesus Christ is in you, except ye be reprobates, 2 Corinthians 13.

I began to pray, "Father in Heaven, IF you are the Potter within my mind, and IF you work through my faculty to create by imagining, how could I ever know such a thing?"

Nothing.

The thoughts stopped.

Relief.

I rolled over and looked at my iPhone – 11:45, March 31, 2023.

As I relaxed, I began to imaging Jonetta and Corban and myself on a beautiful Colorado trail. It was sunny with a cold breeze. I imagined the trail ahead of us… it dropped off about 20 yards ahead so that you couldn't see any more of the trail, and at that moment my old chocolate lab, Guage, appeared in the center of the trail. He ran to us, and we squatted down to greet him. When he reached me, I wrapped my arms around him– tears filled my eyes. The love that I felt for that old dog returned and filled my being. I heard Jonetta say, "He looks just like Guage!" I imagined Jonetta being so happy to see him. I could feel the love and the joy in the embrace. I drifted into sleep within that beautiful image.

We woke the following morning by Corban jumping into our bed. "Get up, Nana! Make me some noodles!" he exclaimed.

The morning was a usual Saturday. We filled book orders, cleaned a little, and ran necessary errands. Jonetta made a light lunch.

Shortly after lunch Corban found me upstairs working on a project. "Paw-paw, Nana wants to go on a hike," he said.

"I can't, Corban. Paw-paw is working," I explained. Corban was disappointed, but didn't press the issue. He went downstairs to tell Nana we couldn't go.

About five minutes passed as I was busy trying to finish my little task, and a thought entered my mind: *Take them on a hike– get away from your problems for a few hours.*

I can't go on a hike. It's cold and I've got a lot to do.

You need to take a hike.

I laughed. Sounded like I needed to get lost, for sure! *Take a hike!*

Alright, alright. I'll get changed.

I'd heard that old people liked to talk to themselves. Well, so much for getting old.

"Let's go up to Castlewood Canyon," I suggested as we jumped into the truck. Corban was buckled in and smiling at me from the back seat.

Jonetta thought about it for a long minute. "How about Cheesman Canyon? We've never been there, and I'd love to see it!"

"Cheesman Canyon?" I'd never heard of it.

"Yeah, it's supposed to be beautiful – come on, let's go!"

It took us almost two hours to get there. She read the sign as we pulled into the lot at the trailhead, "Upper Cheeze Man Canyon Trail!" Jonetta said in a heavy southern drawl, really emphasizing "Cheeze Man", and we burst into laughter. Corban started laughing without knowing why. He thought his Nana talked just fine.

The air was cold and there was a breeze but at least was a sunny day. Jonetta wrapped Corban in a down jacket and sock toboggan for his head. We grabbed our walking sticks and set off on the trail.

Yeah, she was right– it was beautiful! The trail was etched along the side of the mountain around Cheesman Reservoir, with views of the reservoir that look like something from a painting.

We were on the trail headed back toward the truck. It was getting late in the afternoon, but the sun was still bright with no clouds and a cool breeze. There were also very few people that day. The trails in Colorado are normally packed on weekends, so it was unusual to see so few on the trail.

We came around a bend in the trail and it straightened about 30 yards ahead, then disappeared in a drop-slope. Jonetta was a yard ahead and Corban was just behind my feet, when a chocolate lab popped up from the slope. No hikers. No dog owners in sight. Just a chocolate lab…

Dear reader, I swear to you that this is absolutely and completely true. It is without embellishment or exaggeration, and it is written just as it happened: that lab that looked identical to my old lab, Guage, ran down the trail toward us. I realized that I was seeing the scene that I had created within my imagination less than 24 hours before. My vision instantly reduced into a cone. Tunnel vision, as if I were looking at the dog through a rifle scope. Time slowed, and the next few seconds felt like minutes.

He ran toward us as I heard Jonetta say, "Look, look, Michael! He looks just like Guage!" Remember that I had not shared my imaginal creation with Jonetta.

As he drew closer, I squatted down. I didn't squat because I wanted to squat– I didn't have a choice. My legs buckled under me.

He got to me as my knees touched the trail. I wrapped my arms around him and he, this strange dog, seemed genuinely happy to see me. Jonetta squatted to pet him, as well.

"He's got gray whiskers like Guage, too!" she squealed!

How was this happening?

The scene that I'd created in my mind the night before was constructed in real life before my eyes. It was identical to what I saw in my mind's eye.

Tears formed in my eyes.

"Honey, what's wrong with you," Jonetta saw the tears as I hugged the dog.

"I'm okay, I'm okay," I responded. A young couple walked up and apologized for the dog coming to us.

"We're so sorry," said the female hiker.

I stood up to greet them and felt nauseous, but my vision had returned to normal.

"No, no," I responded to the couple, "It's okay, I just don't understand what's happening... I saw this last night." Jonetta looked confused, and so did the hikers.

"You saw this? What do you mean–"

"Look," I interrupted, "I'm a little freaked out right now- no, I'm *really* freaked out right now because I saw this-your dog-last night-on this trail-" I couldn't get it out. It sounded ridiculous, and incoherent. It sounded crazy. *I* sounded crazy.

Jonetta put her hand on my shoulder as if to signal to the hiker's that I was a mentally disabled man who muttered incoherent things to perfect strangers. The dog remained at my feet.

"Ok, nice to meet you," they both said as they rushed up the trail away from the psychopath and his attractive caregiver. It was comical. Yeah, I live in Colorado, but I don't smoke weed.

"Michael–"

"Jonetta, let's get to the truck. I'll tell you in the truck."

<u>15</u>

Can You Believe

Jonetta and I talked all the way home and deep into the night. We talked throughout the following day.

Context was key.

My desire to understand and know Paul's words, *"To whom God would make known what is the riches of the glory of this mystery among the Gentiles; which is Christ in you, the hope of glory* (Col. 1:27)", had begun in 2019, and had grown into an unquenchable fire, and up to that moment on that trail.

Context. All of my studies in combination with some of the hidden texts discussed by Gregg Braden and others, in combination with my fervent and continual prayers, had caused me to blow a gasket.

I had been angry with what had happened regarding our book business, and it brought me to the point of feeling abandoned by God. The event was necessary. The anger was necessary. I was angry, but I sinned not (Eph. 4:26). I vented my anger, then returned to the scriptures and to prayer.

The evening that the thought *"I Am your Potter"* entered in, I searched. The search led me to the creation of the imaginal scene just before sleep.

The "vision", for lack of better words, happened less than 24 hours later.

Contemplating the event on the trail astonished me, as it would have been impossible to create. We had to have been on that trail at exact position and moment to match the scene I'd created in my mind the evening before.

The couple with their dog – a dog that looked identical to our old dog, was the dog in my imaginal scene. Everything had to be at an exact position and time on that trail for all to play out perfectly.

We had to choose *that* specific trail that was approximately two hours away from our home.

The dog owners had to leave their home, wherever that was at, in the precise moment to be on that exact place in the trail so that the imaginal scene would be in perfect concert with our movements.

If we had been a few seconds off either way, it wouldn't have happened.

It's impossible.

It had to be a couple with a dog that looked just like our old dog. The weather had to be cool, with a breeze, and the sky had to be sunny– all to match my imaginal scene.

All of it had to be precisely perfect in every way.

Now I ask you, how does any of this make sense? I am not a 'prophet' or a 'visionary'.

There is only one conclusion when we examine the research, the study, the hours of prayers, my burning desire to know the mystery of Christ, the thought *I Am your Potter*, that God operates from within, and the idea that the Son is our Potter Who uses the creative faculty we commonly and casually refer to as "imagination".

The Potter– the Former and Fashioner– the Creator– was revealing that Jesus Christ works within man through man's mind and man's creative faculty that we refer to as our imaginative power. The wonderful human imagination.

It is certainly not the sole, singular way that Christ works within and through us, but it is without doubt that He works through man's creative mind to create man's reality and future. *As a man thinketh in his heart, so is he* (Prov. 23:7).

To be completely transparent with you, I didn't want to accept it. I'd been happy thinking that He was without, in a place afar off.

Robin Smit, an author who holds a Master's in both Theology and Biblical Studies, in her article titled, "Power of Imagination", said the following:

> The word imagination in the Webster's dictionary says: the faculty or action of forming new ideas, or images or concepts of external objects not present to the senses; it is the ability of the mind to be creative or resourceful [sic].
>
> I think we get a better idea of imagination when we look at it in the Hebrew…
>
> In Hebrew there are two words for imagination… *yatsar and deemyon*. The word *yatsar* is to form, fashion, and purpose. It is to squeeze into shape as a potter does with clay. The word *deemyon* means resemblance, likeness, similarity. The root of the word is *damah* which we see in Genesis 1:27 – we were created in His image and also according to His **likeness** (damah).
>
> I believe we are to use our imagination using the mind of Christ and SEEING (or imagining) in us what He sees. And our mind renews as it co-imagines with Him, and like a potter, we begin to form (yatsar) images, ideas, and concepts by SEEING Him and as a result, SEEING who we really are as image and likeness (damah) of Him. He is whole and complete… therefore we are whole and complete. He is co-seated and we are co-seated. And our mind's eye (our

imagination) begins to SEE these truths about our identity.

In this use of our imagination, we are no longer seeing from a place of lack. In other words, we are no longer seeing that we are sick and IF we can just imagine good health, or imagine Jesus healing us, THEN we will manifest healing. NO….. we see His image and know we are the same image. There is no sickness because His image is whole so therefore we are whole! We are not seeing that we are struggling financially and IF we can imagine being wealthy, getting a new job, receiving a check in the mail, etc., THEN we will manifest these things. NO… the real power of imagination is seeing His image… He is abundant and prosperous in ALL things… therefore we are abundant and prosperous in ALL things!

The key to imagination is: HE is and THEREFORE I am language! This is rest! It's all about Him and what He has done for us, and as us. And from that place of rest the manifestation of our FULL, FINISHED inheritance is effortless [sic]. *Power of Imagination*, Robin Smit, May 18, 2022; Public Blog Post, from from URL: https://itisfinished.blog

For the next year I experimented with the idea because of what transpired on that trail. That "vision" was created in my imagination on the evening of March 31, 2023, and it was set in reality to play out perfectly and identically during the late afternoon of April 1, 2023.

There was no denying it. People could deny it. They might laugh, and scoff, and lose all respect for me as a brother, but there was no denying it.

It was done completely out of my external control, but what happened on that trail was the exact scene that I had imagined– even in the words that Jonetta said in my imaginary creation, she said them that day.

It was as if it were all a great play, with each character having a script, and all played their parts perfectly.

I was coming to the firm belief that what had happened on that trail was *God making known to me the riches of the glory of this mystery among the Gentiles, which was Christ in me.* I didn't necessarily want to believe it, but nothing else made sense in relation to the context.

So, over the course of the next twelve months I prayed and used my creative imagining to form scenes in my mind that depicted the positive, affirmative outcomes of my specific prayers– always asked in His name. Always done within and through love.

I can testify publicly that every prayer over the next twelve months was answered in the way that I had imagined, and in the affirmative, with the exception of only a few prayers where I could not generate and feel the desire fulfilled, or I didn't remain faithful to the end, or in prayers that I was asking for another.

We must understand that when praying for another, they may be imagining failure. They may be looking back, and taking their hands from the plow.

To live in constant anxiety and fear and doubt is to "pray" for such an outcome. Imagining the worst is to pray for the worst.

Paul said, "Pray without ceasing". He was telling us that we are forever in prayer in our mind, as we are continually running our inner dialogue, "thinking and imaging" a future outcome.

Our future is determined by the thoughts and intents of our hearts. *As a man thinketh in his heart, so is he.*

Every prayer that I asked in His name (surrounded myself in the answer and believing that I had received what I asked for, and feeling the wish fulfilled) was received.

His promises are true!

My failures in prayer were a direct consequence to my inability to get the feeling, or to remain faithful to the outcome in spite of the circumstances.

We are the operant power of that Power that works within us only by our obedience and faithfulness to His commands. It is by our faith that we are made whole, and it is by our lack of faith that our prayers go unanswered.

It is on us. It is our responsibility. We are without excuse. We shepherd our sheep; we are the good gardener who faithfully tends to the garden of our mind, or we are the evil gardener who plants bad seed, and who neglects the weeds to our own peril.

These are the true, hidden secrets of the art of prayer.

In sharing this with you, I am a metaphorical Judas, for I am sharing the secret that I have been shown, and revealing His identify and location.

This revelation to you may cause my metaphorical suicide, as my former life may disappear. My ministry and books may be rejected and cast aside because of this revelation, but you must know—

someone must tell you that Jesus Christ is within you, and how He designs your life and answers your prayers is through the righteous use of your imaginal creative power within your mind. If fear prevents me from telling you, then who will tell you? How will you know?

Christ in you is the hope of glory, and the mystery among the Gentiles (Col. 1:27). *Christ, whom we preach, warning and teaching every man in all wisdom, that we may present every man perfect in Christ Jesus* (Col. 1:28).

Am I therefore become your enemy, because I tell you the truth (Gal. 4:16)?

Can you believe that He is not afar off, but that He is really within you?

John said, "*The Word became flesh, and dwelt among us* (John 1:14)." That is a mistranslation. The word translated "among" is the Greek preposition "en" (Strong's, 1722). It is translated properly, "within."

So, when the verse is properly translated, it reads, "*The Word became flesh and **dwelt within us**.*"

It is through our obedience to His gospel and our baptism for the remission of sins that He comes to dwell within us; so, the creative Power that worketh within us is Jesus Christ (Eph. 3:20).

In order for Christ to save all, He dwells within us, and He lives, according to Hebrews 7:25, to make intercession for us.

This is the same Jesus Who by all things were made, and without Him was not anything made that was made (John 1:3).

And because He lives and dwells within us, we can know that all things are possible. Jesus said, *"But with God, all things are possible (Matt. 19:26)."*

If all is possible to God, and God lives within us through His Son, then all things are possible to Him Who is within us. He said, *"If thou canst believe, **all things are possible to him that believeth** (Mark 9:23)."*

Can you believe?

16
Tell Him

I received an email around the first few days of June of this year from a brother in Christ from Arkansas who had read one of my books and decided to reach out in desperation. I share this with his permission on his condition that I wouldn't disclose his true name or the name of the company he works for.

I discovered through our discussions that "Joe" is 38, works first-shift at a plant, and grew up in the church around Little Rock.

Him and his wife, "Jane", had been married thirteen years, and they have a daughter who is 10.

They've always attended church faithfully, and he leads prayer from time and time in worship services.

Joe said their life was "normal". Routine.

He reached out to me via email because he wanted prayer and advice. Why? Jane came to him in November of '23 wanting to separate. She told him that she loved him, but she was no longer "in love" with him. They'd been separated for about seven months at that point.

He admitted that they had grown distant, but didn't know of any serious problems that warranted separation. She left in spite of his attempts to persuade her to stay together and work on their marriage.

Joe said that Jane immediately stopped attending church services, but allowed him to continue to take their daughter. Jane seemed to want nothing to do with Joe after their separation.

He prayed continually and asked the church to pray for them. He shared his frustrations with me, and his perception that God had simply turned His back. He couldn't understand why.

"I've prayed so much, and I've seen no results," he repeated. He admitted that he had lived for a long time with a feeling that he was empty inside, and he felt as though he had been "going through the motions" for several years to this point.

Joe seemed to do everything right. He's been, as far as I could tell, consistent and faithful. Beautiful family, good job, nice home, faithful to the Lord, attends all services, prays regularly… but his life had come apart, and it seemed as though nothing he was doing was having any effect to stop the downward spiral.

"What else can I do?" Joe asked me this question several times throughout the course of our 'back-and-forth' emails. The Lord seemed to be prodding me to share this revelation of prayer with Joe, but I couldn't do it.

Joe is a brother in Christ, and as much as I wanted to share these secrets of prayer, my fear of his reaction upon hearing this strange idea prevented me from telling him. Fear is the enemy.

"I'm praying for you, brother," were the words I said in every email. However, I knew deep down that if Joe continued to imagine the worst, to him it would be given– regardless of the "words" he said in prayer.

Whatever Joe "pictured" in his mind and "believed" in his heart would come to pass, for *as a man thinketh in his heart, so is he.* As within, so without.

But I just couldn't tell him.

I shared our discussions with Jonetta. I admitted to her my fears. I admitted my shame and guilt for being too scared to tell him what I'd recently learned about prayer. I didn't tell him how *we* were experiencing wonderful results.

"You've got to tell him, Michael", Jonetta encouraged, but she knew I wasn't ready.

"He'll think I've left the faith," I protested.

"He won't think any such thing!" she argued.

"It sounds too much like something from a New Age seminar," I countered.

"Michael, stop," she objected. "Hasn't the Lord answered our prayers in impossible ways this past few months?"

"Yeah," I admitted.

"What's so 'New Age'? What? That you've discovered how to actually *do* what Jesus said to do? To feel that you receive what you ask Him for and to *live as if* our prayers are *already answered*? That's the Bible, Michael, and we see the results now as never before! We have the proof!"

"I'm not telling him." I wouldn't budge.

"You're a better man than that," Jonetta responded in anger and frustration.

I received an email from Joe in the third week of June. It contained only one sentence:

"She served me with divorce papers."

"Tell him, Michael!" Jonetta almost shouted after I shared the contents of Joe's email. "Tell him or you might get your own papers," she said as she left the room. Jonetta was close to blowing her top. She watched it play it before her: one brother was losing his family; the other brother was too scared to tell the secret to save the family.

So, I did what any rational man in my position would do. I did what my wife said.

Thank God for a good woman.

Thank God for this wonderful woman.

My email response to Joe was several pages, but I've condensed it here to save space.

I shared with Joe much of what you're reading in this story. I explained Mark 11:24, and my discovery that He, Jesus within us, is our Potter and works within us through our creative, picturing faculty– our imagination, and how we must *feel as if we already have our desire* in order that we may receive our answer, as Mark 11:24 states.

I encouraged Joe to believe that if he could *create the imaginal act in his mind,* and if he could *feel how it would feel to have his prayer answered,* and if he could *hold faithfully to that imaginal vision,* that his faith would make him whole. These three simple steps are the great secret to all successful prayer.

I had recently discovered this great secret, and I was actively using the secret in my prayers. I was

experiencing remarkable answers to my prayers–
answers that the world would deem as "miracles", for I
was, through this great secret, receiving things that
were seemingly impossible.

Two days passed and I heard nothing from Joe.
My anxiety was growing. My fears that Joe would
think that I'd lost my mind seemed to be coming true.

It's been two days.

I blew him out.

Joe's gone.

*I revealed the secret to him... he believes me to
be a religious nut.*

No.

No, he doesn't think that.

I did the right thing.

I took Jonetta's advice.

I did what the Lord wanted me to do.

I shared the idea buried in the scriptures.

Joe received the secret with gladness of heart.

He will contact me.

He will write back.

I was taking my own medicine. I was
"praying" and holding to the desired outcome. I was

forming the desired outcome in my imagination, and Jesus, the Potter and Power that worketh within, would answer.

I got an email from Joe about half-an-hour later!

Joe admitted that my "advice" was something he'd never heard or considered, and it sounded "different", but he was willing to try– he'd do almost anything at that point.

He wanted to save his family.

I advised Joe to mentally disregard the service of the divorce papers, and to, instead, go into his closet and shut the door behind him. Shut out all external senses.

To go and do this one thing– *to forget what was behind, and to reach forth unto that thing which was before him* – that thing he desired most. The salvation of his marriage. To *press toward that mark for the prize of the high calling.*

The answer to Joe's prayer would be the most wonderful gift for him in the here and now (Phil. 3:13-14), so he must ask *in His name – to **believe that he***

had already received it, in *order for him to receive it* (Mark 11:24).

Forget the divorce papers.

Forget that she had said she wasn't in love.

Forget that they hadn't lived together over the past seven months.

Forget the fears of a broken home.

Forget thinking about an undesirable future.

For Joe to be able to "believe that he had already received his answer" would require him to create his imaginal scene that would imply the affirmative answer to his prayer, as if it were already done, and to *feel the feeling of that scene.* He had to imagine a scene that implied that Jane had changed her mind.

Joe needed a miracle.

I instructed Joe to go to sleep in the knowledge, trust, assurance— to fall asleep in the *feeling as if* all was finished, and to fall into sleep *"in that feeling that it was finished"*.

I asked him to tell no one, but to keep his mental, imaginal acts to himself.

I also told him to ask no one for help, as the Lord needs the help of no other man.

I also explained to him that I would, in my own imagination, "hear" him say to me that the Lord had answered his prayers.

Joe and I exchanged cell numbers so that we could text each other, as we'd spoken only through email.

Three days passed...

"Mike! Brother Mike! It's Joe!" said the excited man on the other end of the call.

"Who?" I asked. I didn't recognize the number. It was probably a telemarketing call, but he called me *"brother"*?

"Mike, it's Joe (last name withheld)!"

"Joe! How are you, brother!", I replied. Jonetta had just put Corban to bed, and I looked at the living room clock: 8:15 PM.

"Brother Mike...", and with those words Joe broke down and wept.

Chills sweep through my body as I share with you what Joe told me next.

Joe, after receiving my email, went to the Lord in prayer. He created his imaginal scene and presented it to the Lord.

He admitted to me that it took him a long time to *feel the feeling as if his prayer was already answered*, but he finally got it. He felt it.

He said that when he had finally achieved *the feeling of his wish fulfilled*, he spent an hour thanking and praising God loudly and repeatedly– he couldn't help it.

He explained that on the first night after his prayer, he laid in his bed imagining that Jane was in bed next to him, and he finally fell asleep *"feeling as though she was there in his bed"*. He said he woke through the night and reached across the bed to see if she was there.

Joe admitted that when he woke the following morning, he felt intense fear and doubt, but he said that he countered his fears with gratitude to God, thanking God out loud having answered his prayers. The act neutralized his fears, instilled new confidence, and lifted his mood.

Joe also confessed that he'd never been in such a "mental battle", as he was finding that his mind was reverting back to fear and doubt, but he managed to "keep the birds from building a nest". He managed to

keep his hands to the plow, and didn't look back. He
didn't unfit himself for the kingdom.

For two more nights Joe said he was able to fall
asleep in the feeling of his answered prayer. I was so
proud and impressed by his obedience, because I'd
found in my own experiences that getting the *feeling*
and then *falling asleep in the feeling* can be a
challenge.

On the third day Joe had finished his shift at the
plant and was walking to his truck which was parked
in what he called "the side lot". He said it was close to
4:00 PM.

Jane and their daughter were standing by his
truck. He said that, as he got closer, he could see tears
on Jane's face. He thought that maybe her mom or dad
had died, or maybe she was there to tell him that she
was taking their daughter and moving out of state.

It was none of that.

He told me that Jane threw her arms around
him and told him how sorry she was as she wept on his
shoulder.

She had changed her mind, and no longer
wanted a divorce. She told Joe that she'd experienced
an overwhelming feeling the day before. It was a

sense of renewed desire for him that accompanied a deep craving to reconcile.

Jane felt shame at her core, and a longing to bring her family back together. She couldn't explain why or how.

Joe's imaginal act of seeing his desired outcome, then living in the end as if his prayer was already answered, was given to him by the Lord.

Joe and Jane spent the next few hours moving her clothes and things back into their home, then he called me to share the news.

Joe got his miracle.

Joe didn't fail to meet the test.

Joe's courage and his obedience to the good news that Jesus Christ was within him and Jesus would save him, and his experience of the seeming "miracle that followed" was an undeniable proof of the great secret of Mark 11:24.

Joe had been given the greatest of all gifts, because it was to Joe that *God made known what is the riches of the glory of this mystery among the Gentiles; which is Christ in you, the hope of glory* (Col. 1:27).

17

As Within, So Without

Any presentation of a biblical doctrine must demonstrate that it contains a specific reference to our life in the here and now, as well as in the hereafter, because man is far more concerned with the here and now than with the future.

Therefore, if you would interest anyone in the truth, you must first appeal to the power that they can experience in the here and now. That power is the hidden power within them– Jesus Christ within them (John 1:14), the hope of glory (Col. 1:27).

The gospel– this good news that Jesus Christ is within and that He will give us what we need and desire in the here and now (John 10:10; 3 John 2:2), is almost impossible to believe, but I've found it to be entirely true.

In Joe's case, I presented the idea that Jesus was within and would give him salvation in the here and now (the impossible salvation of his marriage). Joe heard the Word.

Belief in this good news would require Joe to believe in the possibility of salvation (of his marriage) with all of his heart. It would be a degree of belief that would cause him to mentally "turn away" from his existing problem through a radical change of attitude and heart (repentance), and to form within him a new mental image of his desired outcome. Joe then exclaimed within, "Jesus is the Son of God" (confess), and he proceeded to immerse himself within the feeling of his wish fulfilled (baptism).

Joe then, after rising from his previous mental immersion in the feeling of the wish fulfilled, went on his way rejoicing in the fact that Jesus had saved him (Jesus had given him his desire). Joe remained faithful to his imaginal act until the Lord brought it into being. Joe remained faithful unto death– the death of the old man unto the birth of the new.

Joe heard, believed, repented, confessed, was baptized, and remained faithful. He obeyed the gospel.

We find that the process of successful prayer emulates the process of God's plan of salvation.

God's plan of saving the inner man– our soul, requires us to obey these six steps. We see it throughout the New Testament acts of conversions. Jesus said, "*He that believeth and is baptized shall be saved; but he that believeth not shall be damned* (Mark 16:16)," and the entirety of the steps are revealed in the remote text.

This process that we refer to as the plan of salvation is for the eternal salvation of the inner man saving of the inner man– the soul, and we're not ashamed of it because it is the *power of God unto salvation to all that will believe* it (Rom. 1:16)."

Here's the incredibly remarkable and completely extraordinary hidden secret which has been masked, but hidden in plain sight: this outward plan that saves the inner man, the plan of salvation, hides the plan of prayer which is given to save the outer man daily– this process that I refer to as *the hidden secrets of the art of prayer*. To pray successful and to receive our answer to every prayer is to emulate the plan of salvation in our prayer process. It is to **hear** that Jesus is within and that He can and will give us our answer– this is the good news!, Then to **believe** with all of our hearts. Then to go to Him in prayer and *ask in His name*, which means to create via imagination an imaginal scene that implies our desired outcome– this is **repentance**. We, in our imagination, "turn away" from our existing problem and turned "toward Christ's offer". Our mental movement toward immersion into the feeling of the wish fulfilled is to exclaim that Jesus is the Son– that is **confession**. Then as we step into the imaginal act of being surrounded by our answer is to step into the "phycological water" of receiving what we have asked Him for– **baptism into the feeling of the answered prayer**.

When "water" is seen in the scripture, we must also understand that physical water in the scriptures sometimes symbolizes "what is hidden"– the hidden psychological meaning.

Water does also now save us (1 Peter 3:21). Water is the element that used when one obeys the gospel.

In prayer, water becomes a metaphorical element (psychological immersion into the wish fulfilled, or to be surrounded by the answer) which does also now save us (believe that you have received and you will receive, Mark 11:24). This psychological immersion, or baptism, is also not removal of filth from the flesh (1 Peter 3:21), but it is by this immersion into the answered prayer that we give our answer of a good conscience toward God (*Ibid*). It contains this beautiful dual meaning: real, physical water for baptism in our obedience to the gospel; metaphorical water (psychological meaning) for baptism in our obedience to Christ's command regarding prayer (Mark 11:24).

God's plan of salvation as seen in the conversions found in the Book of Acts is one of the Bible's most powerful messages because it is dual in meaning. Let me explain:

Our body is the most magnificent structure in all of creation. It is dual in nature. It is a physical thing comprised of flesh, bone, and blood– an outer being called the carnal man. Outer man: the temple. Esau.

This most magnificent bodily structure called the outer man holds an invisible secret. It holds the most magnificant creation in all the world... our inner man. Our inner man is comprised not of flesh, bone, and blood, but of the essence of God– the soul. This is the inner man. It is Jacob.

The duality of man is to recognize that man is two-fold in design. He is a soul embodied by flesh. He exists as an invisible soul hidden within visible flesh.

As above, so below.

As within, so without.

As without, so within.

247

As a man thinketh in his heart (as within), so is he (so without).

God's plan of salvation is eternal, and is eternity for the inner man, and is performed outwardly and attained through the gospel by hearing, believing, repenting, confessing, being baptized in water, and remaining faithful unto his physical death; therefore, the inner man is eternally saved, and the promise is fulfilled– Jesus brought life (John 10:10). As without, so within.

Prayer, as emulated by what is seen in God's plan of salvation, is temporal for the "daily" salvation of the outer man, and is performed inwardly and is attained through emulating the gospel by hearing, believing, repenting, confessing, being baptized in metaphorical water, and remaining faithful unto the physical death of our problem; therefore, the outer man is temporally saved, and the promise if fulfilled– Jesus brought life more abundantly (John 10:10). As within, so without.

Jesus, the Son of Man, Son of God, lived two-thousand years ago, and died on a cross to save our inner man, our soul.

Jesus, the Son of Man, Son of God, lives now today within you to save your outer man, and to give you this daily life more abundantly. Your body is the cross upon which He lives.

In Joe's case, he was saved eternally when he obeyed the gospel and was baptized in water. He received life. His marriage was saved in the here and now when he obeyed the instructions of true prayer which emulates obeying the gospel by being baptized in metaphorical water. He received life more abundantly.

Sometime during the late first century to mid-second century, a practice developed. The practice was a signal of encouragement to others to remember that Jesus was crucified for you, and He was crucified upon you, and He lives within you.

The signal was performed with the hand, and seen by the act of "painting an invisible cross on self". One would touch their head, then chest, then one shoulder, then the other shoulder. It was the sign of the cross, and intended to say silently, "Jesus is crucified on you."

The signal said that Jesus was hanging on you, the cross, because your spine and collar-bone is the human cross upon which Christ hangs. The skull is where He is entombed– Golgotha, or Calvary (Calva), the skull. The skull houses the man's mind whereby Christ lives, and moves, and has His being (Acts 17:28).

The signal was adopted by the Catholics at the end of the fourth century, and is, as you know, still practiced unto this day.

Neither shall they say, Lo here! or, lo there! for, behold, the kingdom of God is within you (Luke 17:21).

The kingdom is within you.

The kingdom of heaven (above) is within you, in "your above"– in your wonderful mind, the skull that is positioned above all.

Therefore, as you think in your heart (in your skull, the above), so are you (your outer world is created and formed).

You are beginning to understand the power of He who is within you. Paul said, "*Let this mind be in you, which was also in Christ Jesus: Who, being in the form of God, thought it not robbery to be equal with God* (Phil. 2:5-6)."

Our modern minds have been steeped in the wisdom of this world, and when we experience such a miraculous answer to prayer, as Joe did, our mind attempts to "reason" within itself through the template of worldly wisdom. Our mind attempts to discredit the Lord's answer in opposing thoughts, such as, "It would have happened anyway." Our mind will, upon seeing the prayer fulfilled, attempt to discount the event.

It would have happened anyway. These thoughts are from the Adversary who is called "The Accuser" (Rev. 12:10). He continually accuses us before our God day and night.

There may be not better words that speak of this principle than Paul's words in 2 Corinthians 10:4-6:

> *For the weapons of our warfare are **not carnal**, but mighty through God to the pulling down of strong holds; Casting down **imaginations**, and every high thing that exalteth itself against the knowledge of God, **and bringing into captivity every thought to the obedience of Christ**; And having in a readiness to revenge all disobedience, when your **obedience is fulfilled**.*

Therefore pick up your cross and follow after
Him.

Imagine the very best.

He is within you.

Today is the day of salvation.

18

No Coincidences

David is new friend from Oklahoma. He is a retired cop, a minister of the gospel, and a man who is as rock-solid as I've ever seen. The church is being made better for having him in service.

David's love and encouragement has not only been a boon to our faith, but he caught something in the scripture that I hadn't seen myself.

We've been discussing this story and the concepts herein, and David said, "Brother Mike, the concept [of Mark 11:24] is seen in the action of the Shunammite woman in 2 Kings."

"I'm ashamed to admit that I can't recall it," I admitted to David. He got his Bible, found the text, and began to explain...

Elisha had told a woman that she was to have a child, and she had a son. Then the boy died (2 Kings 4:20).

The woman journeyed back to Elisha who was at Mt. Carmel, and when Elisha saw her coming, he told his servant to run and "*to meet her, and say unto her, Is it well with thee? is it well with thy husband? is it well with the child* (v. 26)?"

David brought me to the last part of that verse, which is the key:

"And she answered, It is well (Ibid)."

Understand that her son had already, at this point, died; however, I hope you won't miss what I had missed in the past. She answered, "*It is well*".

Why did she journey back to the man of God?

Because she encountered the pinnacle of a mother's grief– the death of her child.

Within every problem lies the solution. The solution is found within your desire.

What was the woman's desire?

She wanted her son back.

Her desire brought her back to the man of God. We, like her, are brought back to Jesus, the Son of God, time and time again as we're confronted by life's challenges. And within our problem lies the solution as it comes forth within us masked as "desire".

We see the drama unfold as she comes to the man of God; verse 27:

> *And when she came to the man of God to the hill, she caught him by the feet: but Gehazi came near to thrust her away. And the man of God said, Let her alone; for **her soul is vexed within her**: and the Lord hath hid it from me, and hath not told me.*

When we come to the Son of God in prayer, we "catch Him by His feet", as *feet* in the scripture symbolize "understanding" and "discernment". So to start at the foot, or to desire the foot, or to grab hold of the feet means to desire wisdom and understanding and the ability to judge with righteous (right thinking) judgment.

We find in the rest of the story that the man of God brought her son back to life (vv. 28-37). The man of God gave to her that which seemed impossible– the answer to her desire.

The woman, when confronted with unbearable grief, discovered her desire.

To whom did she go?

She returned to the man of God.

Why go to him?

Because she knew that he had the power to grant her petition. She believed with all of her heart.

That belief moved her back toward the man of God. She caught him at the feet– she wanted understanding and wisdom to know what she must do to be saved from the death of her child.

Her desire and recognition that the man of God could save her moved her toward him– this is symbolic of prayer our willingness to go to the Lord in prayer.

Her deceptive response, "*It is well* (2 Kings 4:26)," indicates that she was confessing that her prayer was already answered. She was affirming that her desire was already received.

Therefore I say unto you, **What things soever ye desire**, *when ye pray,* **believe that ye receive them**, *and ye shall have them* (Mark 11:24)."

The woman's son was dead, but she said, "*It is well*". The bridge of incident was constructed– her answer had already been given. She needed only to believe, and to move across the path of belief toward her desired outcome.

Her faith made her whole. Her son lived!

Beat your plowshares into swords and your pruninghooks into spears: **let the weak say, I am strong** (Joel 3:10)."

Whenever you are confronted with a problem, go back to the man of God, the Son of God. And whatever you desire, pray, and believe you receive.

All is well.

I am strong.

And in doing so, your son will live again; your faith will make you whole.

It was no coincidence that David reached out to me and became my friend. It is no coincidence that he sees what is hidden within the text. These facts should reveal more to you than what is being said.

Jesus Christ within *you* is working all things together for *your good*, at this very moment, and through His people, his body.

19

The Baby
and the Bath Water

I have made a serious mistake, and I admit that it's taken me over thirty years to realize it. But I confess my error in the hope that you will learn from my mistake in order to save yourself potential heartache... and to be able to receive your every prayer answered.

Many years ago, in 1988, I recognized how emotions may lead one astray. I read Jeremiah 17:9, "*The heart is deceitful above all things, and desperately wicked: who can know it?*" I saw how the televangelists of the day used emotionalism to stir up the crowds which seemed to result in millions of dollars of income for the televangelist's ever-expanding fortunes.

I saw the need to separate emotionalism from the scriptures, and to approach the Bible with reason, and intellect, and proper discernment. My aim was honest, and my desire was sincere.

But I was, at that time, immature. I was without the wisdom that accompanies long life.

In my effort to separate emotionalism from my examination of the Word, I mistakenly conflated "empty or temporary emotionalism" with the positive emotions of faith, hope, and love. I didn't discern that Bible faith was intertwined with feeling.

My immature mind told me to reject all emotion– to avoid and to suppress and to disconnect from any emotion or feeling which might be perceived in the scripture. I became a spiritual "lawyer", seeking only to memorize "the law" so that I could contend for the faith once delivered to the saints, and to destroy all "false teachers" with my cold and sterile knowledge.

However, in doing so, I disconnected my willingness to feel "spiritually". I ran away at any thought of "emotions" brought on by the Word.

I cringed when others spoke of the Holy Spirit

Only televangelists talk about the Holy Spirit.

The thought made me run the opposite direction.

Years of living within these thoughts turned me into a cold, harsh "lawyer" of the Word. I'd become a Pharisee– I was a man who knew the Law, but I was without love for my neighbor.

Though I could speak with the tongues of men and angels, and I could quote the scriptures as well as any seasoned preacher, but I had not love. I became as sounding brass. A tinkling cymbal.

I thought I had faith that could remove mountains, but I didn't have love. I became nothing.

Love bears all things, believes all things, hopes all things, and endures all things, but I had not love.

I speak for no one but myself.

No one made me that way.

That wasn't the teaching of Christ, nor was it the teaching of the church.

That wasn't the teaching of Randall.

It was my mistake. My serious error in judgment.

I, in my effort to separate emotion from reason toward obtaining an above-average knowledge of the Word, threw out all emotion, and feelings, and biblical love.

I hadn't realized that I was throwing out the most important thing of all... love.

In my effort to throw out emotionalism, I threw out love, and I threw out my ability to "feel".

I threw out the baby with the bath water.

That they should seek the Lord, if haply they might feel after him, and find him (Acts 17:27). Dear reader, may I tell you from decades of experience:

when a man kills his feelings long enough, it becomes almost impossible to *feel after the Lord* again.

So now faith, hope, and love abide, these three; but the greatest of these is love (1 Cor. 13:13)."

Faith– you must be able to *feel* if you are to ever accomplish obedience in prayer; for you must *believe that you have received your answer* to prayer to be able to receive (Mark 11:24), and *believing is feeling the answer of your wish fulfilled.*

That faith that moves mountains is that faith that makes you whole, and it requires the ability to feel. Hope– that real, tangible, palatable hope that's produced by faith originates in one's ability to feel, for if you can feel your wish fulfilled, hope comes forth. Hope is a fruit of faith, and faith comes by feeling.

Love– the greatest of the three is the nuclear bomb of all human emotion. God is love. God IS love. Love is, therefore, the eternal emotion. Love's very nature– its essence, is eternal. Love cannot be destroyed, as it is eternal, and whatever is eternal is not destructible. Love is the driving force of all that is good. Love is the main-spring which brings forth all mankind. It is by, through, and for love which man takes a wife, and within which he completes the

creative act of planting the seed. Love compels a
mother to give her life for her child. Love compels a
man to give his life for his family.

Everything else will pass away, but love never
passes away; it never fails.

Love never ends.

Drain some water before you throw it out– your
baby might be in there.

20

Feeling is the Secret

"*Let us hold fast the confession of our hope without wavering, for He who promised is faithful* (Heb. 10:23)."

It is our Father through His Son Jesus Christ who must, without a shadow of doubt, receive the credit, the honor, the glory, the praise, with all thanksgiving to Jesus Christ. Let no other receive praise, and let no flesh glory in His presence.

Not by might nor by power, but by My Spirit, says the Lord of hosts (Zech. 4:6). It's not necessary to share more.

What's necessary is to reiterate what may be, in my opinion, the most important part of how to obey Christ's words in Mark 11:24, as it's written, "*Therefore I say unto you, What things soever ye desire, when ye pray, **believe that ye receive them**, and **ye shall have them**.*"

Believe that you receive them (past tense), and you shall have them (future tense). It is a conditional commandment that appears to be conditioned solely upon our willingness to believe that we receive them.

You must believe that you have received **to** receive. Your internal confession that you have received is made unto, or in the direction of, salvation (receiving your answer).

This concept stands in opposition to logic, reason, and visible reality– it looks like foolishness.

It is written, "*For the preaching of the cross is to them that perish **foolishness**; but unto us which are saved it is the power of God. For it is written, I will **destroy the wisdom of the wise**, and will **bring to nothing the understanding of the prudent*** (1 Cor. 1:18-19)."

To the prudent, the concept of believing that you have received something that you have not yet received, and to do so in order to receive your request isn't prudent or wise.

We are told by the wise men of this world that we must be rational and prudent in order to spare and preserve our lives; however, Jesus said that *whosoever will save his life shall lose it: and whosoever will lose his life for my sake shall find it* (Matt. 16:25).

But His conditional command begs the question: how? How is a man or woman expected to believe that we have received what we have not yet received in order to receive what we desire, so that our faith will make us whole?

'*Feeling as if*' is the answer to the question.
It's seen as a metaphor in Matthew 9:20-21:

And, behold, a woman, which was diseased with an issue of blood twelve years, came behind him, and touched the hem of his garment: for she said within herself, If I may but touch his garment, I shall be whole.

We imagine within prayer that we feel as if our prayer is already answered, and that we have received (past tense) our petition. Such imagining results in a feeling of relief– satisfaction, and it is in *that feeling* that we metaphorically "touch the hem of His garment".

The secret is revealed in Acts 17, but we miss it because we've never been told of this hidden method. It's hiding in plain sight, as it is written, "*That they should seek the Lord, if haply they might **feel after him**, and find him, though he **be not far** from every one of us: For **in him we live, and move, and have our being**; as certain also of your own poets have said, For we are also **his offspring*** (vv. 27-28)."

Feel after the Lord.

The Lord is our being, and if He does indeed operate as our *Potter* through the faculty of mind and our imagining faculty, then it is through the use of the gift of imagining that we accomplish His command to believe that we have received our prayer. Obedience requires the active, loving use of our imaginative faculty.

The use of our imagining faculty is absolutely necessary to experience the feeling that our prayer is answered, as the feeling of relief and satisfaction **before we receive** can only be generated through or use of the imaginal faculty.

Our Lord works His mysteries by and through an assortment of venues and modalities, and we cannot know His ways, just as Isaiah wrote:

> *For my thoughts are not your thoughts, neither are your ways my ways, saith the Lord. For as the heavens are higher than the earth, so are my ways higher than your ways, and my thoughts than your thoughts* (55:8-9).

We could not have known "how" the Lord was working to save Joe and Jane's marriage, and none of us have the wisdom or ability to work all things together to achieve that desired outcome. Jesus said, "*I am Alpha and Omega, the beginning and the ending, saith the Lord* (Rev. 1:8)." We who come to Jesus with our desire of salvation through our answered prayer find that He is the beginning and the end; therefore, we bring our desire to Him (the beginning), we imagine the desired outcome (the end), and hold fast to our faith in that end.

We receive what we ask Him for by living in the end (holding faithfully to the outcome) without ever knowing, or worrying about "how" it is being accomplished, nor should we ever concern ourselves with the Lord's progress of the thing.

I am the beginning and the end; therefore, we're not to concern ourselves or others with any thought to the "middle".

He will work all things together for your good *if* you hold fast to the end, and if believe without wavering. If we do so, we'll see, "*It is finished*".

It is in *getting the feeling that your prayer is answered* that is the critical secret.

21
Hidden Plan

I ask you, with all that has been said now firmly in position, an honest question:

Will Jesus Christ save the soul who obeys His plan of salvation?

While we know His plan of salvation well, and few need any "review", it's important to have it placed in print because I am going to make a bold and unusual statement relating to the plan of salvation, so I pray you'll follow closely.

We find in the New Testament a method by which God saves mankind, also called God's plan of salvation. This plan contains commands via statements and examples wherein man obtains salvation upon his obedience to God's commands.

The steps, or actions, seen in God's plan of salvation are replete in the New Testament, and are listed as follows:

Mankind hears the message that he has sin. Sin is simply "to miss the mark". Man is living in a condition whereby he has missed the mark, and dying in this state is to live in an eternal state absent of God– the state of Hell.

Man must hear that God sent His only Son, Jesus Christ, to die in man's place as a substitution for man's sin – as the Atonement, or sacrifice for man, which redeems mankind from his sins resulting in man's inheritance as a child of God, and the inheritance of an eternal home with God. That's the good news, also called the gospel (Rom. 10:13; Jo. 6:44-45).

When man hears this gospel, he must believe this message and that Jesus is the Son of God (Jo. 3:16; 1 Jo. 4:10); there is no other name whereby a man must be saved (Acts 4:10). Belief alone does not save.

Man must then ascend to the next step, which is repentance. The word means to engage in a radical change of thinking. Man must recognize his sin, then turn away from all sin. It is to "turn away from". Man removes all mental attention, focus, and activity away from sin (Acts 2:38; 17:30). Repentance alone does not save.

Man must speak with his mouth that he believes that Jesus Christ is the Son of God, as this confession is made with the mouth unto, or in the direction of, salvation (Rom. 10:9-10; Acts 8:37). Confession alone does not save.

Man, then moves into water, and is immersed, or baptized, into and under the surface of water for the remission, or the "hiding", of his past sins (Acts 2:38; Acts 22:16; 1 Pet. 3:21). Immersion moves one from the present world into the body of Christ; therefore, he is newly created in Christ (2 Cor. 5:17; Gal. 3:26-27). Immersion alone does not save.

Man, upon being a new creature, must now hold fast to the gospel message, and as a new creation. He must not turn back to his former sins, as he must not remove his hands from the plow. He must look forward and live by "right-thinking", or righteousness, and do so faithfully until the death of his body in this present world (Col. 1:21; Rev. 2:10).

The entirety of this plan of salvation has been hotly debated throughout the ages – to the point of war. Mankind has, upon and by the Great Record, divided and warred against each other.

The severe disagreements and subsequent wars have resulted in numerous divisions of those who profess their belief that Jesus Christ is the Son of God.

Believers who subscribed to their individual set of agreed upon elements denominated themselves into sects; those sects further evolved into what became to be known as religious denominations.

The denominations are recognizable by their adherence to, or rejection of, specific elements of the plan of salvation. Some elements of the plan are deemed by them as "non-essential". In other words, mankind is saved "before" or "without" some of the elements of the plan of salvation. Baptism is a popular element that is deemed as "non-essential" by some groups.

This is a book about prayer. This book is not about denominations and their differences.

But the entirety of the plan of salvation is critical to the statement that I am about to make.

I assert and strongly contend that the entirety of the plan of salvation– the plan by which mankind is given eternal life in the hereafter, contains the hidden plan of all successful prayer.

I further assert that God's plan of prayer as disclosed herein closely emulates His plan of salvation. In other words, the successful steps of proper, effective prayer emulate, or parallel, God's plan of salvation.

The gift of prayer and the hidden secrets for successful prayer are buried within the plan of salvation, and it has been hidden in plain sight throughout the ages.

God's plan of salvation is God's gift of Jesus Christ to all mankind, so that mankind may have life– eternal life in the hereafter (after death).

I contend that God's plan of salvation reveals God's plan of successful prayer to all mankind that he may have life– life more abundantly in the here and now.

The plan of prayer, or the methods of the process of successful prayer toward salvation (our answer received) is seen in God's plan of salvation, itself.

The plan of prayer is His plan and process for saving mankind from every challenge and problem and difficulty man faces in the here and now.

God's plan of salvation through Jesus Christ is the fulfillment of Christ's statement in John 10:10, "*I am come that they might have life* (John 10:10; first part)"; and God's plan of prayer through Jesus Christ is the fulfillment of Christ's statement of the second part, "*and* [*I am come*] *that they might have it* [life] *more abundantly* (John 10:10, second part)."

<u>22</u>

What is Hidden
is Revealed

Man is a dual being.

He consists of the outer man, which is his flesh and blood being, and he consists of the inner man– a being which is invisible and hidden from sight, which is his mind or spirit– his soul.

Man's outer being will die and return to the earth (decay); however, man's inner being will continue, as man is a spirit– a soul.

It is written that man will, after death, be received into eternal life (Heaven), or be cast into outer darkness (Hell); therefore, the soul will continue on in one of two places.

The Bible states these facts plainly.

The Bible contains, as Paul said, what are called allegories (Gal. 4:24). An allegory is a story, poem, or picture that can be interpreted to **reveal a hidden meaning**, typically a moral or political one.

God's plan of salvation is both literal, as it reveals what is required for eternal life; but it's also allegory in that it hides the process of successful prayer.

Prayer must emulate God's plan of salvation, as seen in the stories, parables, examples, and statements made by Jesus Christ (i.e., The Ten Lepers; Luke 17:11-19).

Successful prayer employed by emulating (obeying) the hidden element result in your receiving your answer to your every petition.

Can your Potter, the Power within, be used in evil and destructive ways? Yes, it can, and I'll cover that in a later chapter.

Remember that answer to prayer is a spiritual blessing found in Christ in heavenly places. It is a pearl of great price encased within the exterior shell of virtue. Only the virtuous– only those who have clothed themselves with Christ (Gal. 3:27) should have access to the pearl, and those "so clothed" do offer their petitions based in love and in alignment with Him.

I assert that this specific and hidden method of prayer– God's plan of prayer, is hidden within God's plan of salvation, and it is revealed and interpreted by the Bible, as the Bible interprets itself by the remote text.

I'll show you the hidden secrets in the art of prayer.

MAN'S CONDITION: SIN

In the story of the ten lepers, those with leprosy had been cast into the outer regions of the city, as they couldn't "lawfully" reside within for the risk of contagion.

They were filled with, and living in, sin. Their disease was a metaphor to sin. They had missed the mark, and were living in a state of isolation, loneliness, weakness, pain, anxiety, depression– *hell*.

They were conscious of their condition in this state– *hell*.

They had no hope– *hell*.

God was, to them, absent; therefore, they were condemned to live in this state of "absence from God"– *hell*.

All of these conditions comprised their prison sentence– *hell*.

Those poor and wretched men were living a life of *hell on earth*– a state none want to occupy.

Their desire was salvation. Salvation to them was healing. They desired to be healed of their disease (dis-ease); they desired salvation from their "sin".

Salvation meant a return of health, which in turn meant a return to their families whom they loved, a restoration of their reputations and identities, an opportunity to return to the work of their hands and to the possibility to be productive providers.

Salvation meant that they could attend the Temple– to be in the presence of God.

Salvation meant "heaven" for these men– to be lifted from their current *hell on earth* into a metaphorical heaven on earth– a restoration of their lives.

This is mankind's condition. He is in sin.

THE MESSAGE OF GOOD NEWS

In whom is salvation found?

The ten lepers had a desire to be healed.

They had heard of Jesus, the Master, as seen by their response upon encountering Him. They had, evidently "heard" (to hear) of the Word. It seems that they had also heard that the Master could heal them.

Jesus is salvation. He is the Word. The Word became flesh, and the Word was with God, and the Word was God. The Word has the power to heal– to bring life more abundantly.

This fact is brought to all who sincerely seek God, for He is a rewarder to those who diligently seek Him. He will send Jesus Christ to those who have "heard" the Word, as we find that God sent Christ to the lepers– He appeared to them without warning. God sent His Son to the lost and perishing.

They heard the Word.

The first hidden meaning in the plan of prayer which emulates the plan of salvation is to <u>hear</u> that Jesus has the power to save you in the here and now– to answer your prayer. His wish for you is that you prosper and be in good health. Life more abundantly.

HEAR this good news. Have you heard that Jesus hears your prayers? Will you **hear** this good news?

BELIEVE

The ten lepers, standing afar off from Him, saw Him and recognized Him as Jesus, the Master!

They, in their fear of His wrath due to their current condition of "living in sin" exclaimed, "Have mercy on us!"

The lepers did not petition the Master for cleansing, nor did they beg of Him to save them from their *hell on earth–* they reacted in fear for a simple plea of mercy.

Men living in sin naturally react to Jesus Christ with fear, as they realize when confronted with Jesus of their need for mercy over everything else at that moment, for *He is able to cast both body and soul into Hell.*

The lepers response demonstrated that they had heard of His power. Jesus Immanuel Christ (Isa. 7:14; Matt. 1:23). His names mean: God saves, God with us, the Anointed.

Jesus Christ's response to the lepers represents several unspoken implication which all represent what is hidden, which we will cover.

The second hidden meaning in the plan of prayer which emulates the plan of salvation is to <u>believe</u> that Jesus has the power to save you in the here and now– to answer your prayer. His wish for you is that you prosper and be in good health. Life more abundantly.

BELIEVE this good news. Do you **believe** that Jesus will answer your prayers? Will you **believe** this good news?

REPENTANCE

"Go shew yourselves unto the priests," commanded Jesus.

The step required after belief in God's plan of salvation is "repentance". Jesus said, "*I tell you, Nay: but, except ye repent, ye shall all likewise perish* (Luke 13:3)."

His response to the lepers was for them to repent– hidden within the command of the single word, "*Go*" (Luke 17:14).

For these ten to obey the command to "go" required them to "turn from their present sin". For them to "go" required them to first "turn away from their encampment at the outer edges– their place of sin," and to "turn toward God". This "turning" is the meaning of repentance.

When mankind comes to grips with his current state of *hell on earth* – his sin, he may choose to remain in that state, or he may choose to turn away from that state– to repent.

Unless he repents, or turns via radical transformation of his thoughts and attitudes and beliefs, he will perish in his state of sin.

The third hidden meaning in the plan of prayer which emulates the plan of salvation is to <u>repent</u>. Belief causes the soul to turn toward God, which is to repent. The step after belief is to repent. Jesus commands you to repent– to turn from your present state, and turn toward God so that He may save you in the here and now– to answer your prayer. His wish for you is that you prosper and be in good health. Life more abundantly.

REPENT and turn yourself toward the good news. Will you **repent** and turn yourself away from sin, and toward this good news?

CONFESSION

We must remember that in this story of the ten lepers, we are speaking of a physical healing. This specific text, Luke 17:11-19, doesn't explicitly address God's plan of salvation as seen in the conversions of Acts, but the story hides the components found within God's plan of salvation that instruct us in his plan of prayer to receive our answer to prayer in the here and now.

Christ commanded the lepers, "Go shew yourselves unto the priests" (Luke 17:14). There is hidden within His command several implications.

The leper's obedience to Christ's command also contains hidden components of the plan of prayer.

With prayer in view, Christ commands to go and show the priests.

In this action the leper's were required to believe that they were healed, and to "confess" that they had believed in Jesus Christ– a confession that would be required of them by the priests, for the priests would have demanded, "Who healed you?"

They realized that they would be required to, in view of their healing, make a public confession of their faith in Jesus Christ which made them whole.

This is a hidden and rarely seen component buried within the context of the story– it is an unspoken element.

Therefore, the leper's faith that made them whole demanded their public confession: Jesus Christ is the Son of God and He is the One Who removed my sin!

In the hidden art of successful prayer, we emulate confession within our prayer, and for all time that follows our prayer.

We confess our belief that He is the Son of God to Him within prayer by our imaginal act, for in our obedience to engage in the active use of our imaginal faculty, we thereby proclaim that Jesus Christ is working within us through our imaginal activity.

When we rise from prayer and *live in the end– to live as if we have received our answer* is to tell the world Who answered us. We will, upon receiving our answer, announce our belief that Jesus Christ is the Son of God!

Just as the priests were to make their public confession, we tell the church, and all who will listen of this most incredible good news– that Jesus Christ is the Son of God, and He is within!

The fourth hidden meaning in the plan of prayer which emulates the plan of salvation is to confess. After turning away from sin and turning toward God (repentance), we move toward the priests and prepare ourselves to make the public confession that Jesus is the Son of God.

Confession is made unto salvation. You will confess upon your glorious reception of your answered prayer, as nothing will hold you back– nothing will stop you from telling all of the glorious Son of God Who you've found within upon experiencing your reward– your answer to prayer.

His wish for you is that you prosper and be in good health. Life more abundantly.

CONFESS your belief that Jesus Christ is the Son of God, and that He is within– for Christ within you is the hope of glory. Will you **confess** unto salvation of this good news?

BAPTISM: IMMERSION– BE SURROUNDED

Effective, successful prayer demands that *"when ye pray, **believe that ye receive them** (Mark 11:24)."*

When we engage our imaginative function and create a scene within us– a scene that implies our answered prayer, we begin to feel as if our prayer is answered. This is our obedience to "believe that ye receive them".

To feel as if is to surround ourselves in our answer. We envelop ourself within our prayer via our imaginal creation. This "surrounding", or "enveloping" of our answered prayer is to be immersed, or metaphorically baptized, into our answers. This immersion produces the feeling that our prayer is already answered. This immersion allows us to obey His command to "believe that ye receive them", because when we are immersed in our answer we experience the belief that we have received what we have asked Him for.

Rising from our prayer is to be "wet" with the feelings of relief and satisfaction, due to our belief that we have received what we have asked; therefore, we rise from prayer (immersion in the feeling of the wish fulfilled) rejoicing, as the Eunuch rejoiced when he came up out of the water (Acts 8:39).

The ten lepers did, by their commencement toward the temple and subsequent journey, "immerse themselves in the belief that they had been cleansed– forgiven, healed, saved".

The fifth hidden meaning in the plan of prayer which emulates the plan of salvation is to be baptized– immersed. You must immerse yourself in the feeling of the wish fulfilled, which is to be surrounded in your answer.

Jesus commands you to be immersed into your answer, and be surrounded in the answer to your prayer, as He commanded, *"believe that ye receive them, and ye shall have them* (Mark 11:24)."

BE BAPTIZED and be surrounded, feeling as if your wish is fulfilled, thereby receiving your answer to your every prayer.

This is the most wonderful news– it is the good news of Jesus Christ.

FAITHFUL UNTO DEATH: YOUR CROWN OF LIFE

Your faith will make you whole, and you must remain faithful to Jesus Christ and His promise to give you the answer to your prayer.

You must live as if your prayer is answered until He brings it into your reality. This action is to be "faithful unto death"– the death of your problem.

You, upon rising from the "baptism" done within prayer, open your eyes with the substance of what you hope for– the evidence of something not seen. This is faith, and it is the faith that makes you whole.

It is *the way.*

You now commit yourself to "living as if", meaning that you live as if you have already received your answer to your prayer.

Living as if brings you into that state of peace that surpasses all understanding (Phil. 4:7). You've put your hands to the plow (Luke 9:62). And even though you have not yet apprehended, you believe that you've already received. This confidence causes you to forget those things which are behind as you reach forth to those things which are before you. You press toward the mark of the prize (Phil. 3:13-14)– the appearance of the answer of your prayer.

You must, in this great goal, remain faithful unto death (unto the death of your problem). Do so and you will receive a crown of life (your answer to your prayer).

You will, as in Joe's case, forget the divorce papers and know that she is sleeping next to you. Do this, and in a few days, she will appear at your truck with tears on her cheeks.

To achieve your every prayer answered, you see and employ the hidden secrets in the art of prayer. They are contained in God's plan of prayer as seen in His plan of salvation:

Hear that Jesus is within and has the power to answer.

Believe that He will answer your prayer.

Repent from your current problem.

Confess that He has answered.

Baptism – be immersed into your answer.

Faithful – live as if your prayer is received until it is received.

Dear reader, test it and see.

Do you not realize that Jesus Christ is in you?

Prayer is the act whereby man, being compelled by circumstances, offers petition via mental intervention to God; God, in response, intervenes in the circumstances of man to fulfill man's petition.

—Author

<u>23</u>

Live in the End

Your beginning starts in the end. You must learn what it means to live in the end, for the end is your beginning.

The secret components in the hidden art of prayer, and realizing your objective that your every prayer is answered is to learn to live in the end.

What does it mean to live in the end?

This is clearly seen in the story that we've already discussed– the ten lepers. Let's bring the story into present tense, first person:

You are one of the ten.

As you contemplate your life of pain and isolation, you need not be told what you should desire. Your desire is automatic. You desire healing.

As you realize your greatest desire– to be cleansed of leprosy, you are confronted with the impossibility.

How could you possibly be healed?

It's not possible for you to know how.

Then you hear of a man called Jesus. Someone has said that there is no other name under the heavens whereby you must be healed. Jesus is the Healer.

Your desire to be healed moves you to seek Jesus.

"Oh, if I could only meet Jesus, He would heal me of my leprosy!" your mind exclaims.

Hope is ignited within your being. That hope acts as a main-spring of action which moves you to pray, "My God, my God, please let me meet Jesus!"

You and nine others with leprosy gather together the following morning in prayer. In moments Jesus approaches your group.

"Have mercy on me, Lord!" you exclaim as you see Him.

"Go and show yourself to the priest," He says confidently with love.

You are now, at this very moment, confronted by Him who presents you with a choice – assume He has healed you by obeying His command to go and show the priest, or reject Him and remain where you are. Remain in your *hell on earth*. Remain in sin.

To accept His free gift, you must go and show the priest. Obeying His command requires you to accept His words through an assumptive belief that you are healed. It is to believe, without any evidence and without any proof that your circumstances have change. Your skin is still covered with leprosy.

However, His command requires that you now have your desire.

You must act in faith in the implied assumption that you are now healed.

You rise with your assumption firmly in place, walking without evidence that you are a new creature in Jesus Christ.

You move confidently in the direction of the Temple, toward the priests, and in obedience to Jesus' command.

Your heart exclaims, "I am healed!"

You walk toward the priest with these exclamations in spite of having no physical evidence of any healing. It is unreasonable and illogical, but He said to go. It is *the way*.

As you now journey toward the priest, a substance of your hope forms– literal evidence of what was formerly unseen now appears in reality.

You look at your skin and you are healed!

You, in your uncontrollable joy run back to Jesus exclaiming, "Thank you, Lord, thank you, Lord– I am healed!"

He, in a most beautiful smile, replies, *"Go thy way, your faith has made you whole."*

What was the end?

The end was your healing.

You begin at the end.

You are immersed (baptized) in your answer.

Your faith made you whole.

You hear the Word, believe the Word, accept His free gift, make a radical change in your thinking (repentance) that you now have your desire, immerse your mind and heart into the assumptive belief that you have received your answer (healing) by surrounding and enveloping yourself in the answered prayer (generating the feeling of your answered prayer), and living as if it is finished (walking toward the priest to show yourself to him).

Your journey to the priest is the metaphor – live in the end. Go and show the priests!

You have your desire.

You've received your desire.

Live in the end.

Can you learn to live in the end?

Living in the end is the faith that moves mountains. It is the hope that transforms your present problems into your desired reality. It produces the love that brings the joy which makes our gladness full.

Faith, hope, and love; love is the greatest of these.

You have a problem and contemplate it from within. A desire for a solution to your problem forms from within. You are confronted by the idea of salvation from your problem– Jesus approaches within. You hear His command to assume that you have your answer to your problem from within. You make your choice to either believe that you have received or not believe that you have received– from within. You accept that you now have received from within. You rise and move confidently in your belief that He has saved you from within. As you walk confidently in the direction of your answered prayer, your faith in Him and His answer comes from the unseen into the seen. Your prayer is answered– your faith has made you whole!

Live in the end.

As you move toward the priests, confidently walk in in the assumptive belief that you are healed.

Others moving by may mock and laugh, "Look at you, leper! You are filled with disease!"

The external world and all external circumstance will assault you with the "facts"– it doesn't yet appear that He has answered your prayer.

Fear and doubt attack your mind. You remember that your mind is a garden, and the seed was planted.

Protect the seed!

Tend to your garden.

Continue to walk toward the Temple.

Pain caused by your leprosy hinders your journey. The pain is still there– didn't He heal me? Why am I in such pain? Fear and doubt attack your mind. You remember that your mind is a garden, and He planted the seed.

Protect the seed!

Tend to your garden.

Continue to walk toward the Temple.

Your nine friends who journey with you begin to murmur and complain, "I am in pain and others mock us– where is His salvation? We check our bodies again and again, but we see no healing!"

Fear and doubt attack your mind. You remember that your mind is a garden, and He planted the seed.

Protect the seed!

Tend to your garden.

Continue to walk toward the Temple.

The mocking from others, the pain, the murmuring and complaining, and the lack of faith in your friends brings questions from within:

Why am I not healed?

What will happen if we arrive at the temple and the priest sees our leprosy?

Will I be again rejected?

Will I be executed? Will I suffer greater shame and humiliation?

Fear and doubt attack your mind. You remember that your mind is a garden, and He planted the seed.

Protect the seed!

Tend to your garden.

Continue to walk toward the Temple.

As you journey along to show the priest, you remove your mental attention from all external influences. You ignore the mockers, you ignore your pain, and you ignore the murmurs from your associates. You remove your attention from the lions seeking to devour you, and you place your attention on

He who is within, for He that is in your is greater than He who is in the world.

Your fear and doubt evaporate as you increase your faith from within.

"Look, look! Look at him!" exclaims the nine who travel with you.

"He is healed!" they proclaim as they all surround and examine you.

Your faith has made you whole.

This is *the way*.

*Because strait is the gate, and narrow is **the way**, which leadeth unto life, and few there be that find it* (Matthew 7:14).

*I am **the way**, the truth, and the life: no man cometh unto the Father, but by me* (John 14:6).

Living in the end is to live in the assumptive belief. This is the meaning of Christ's words in Mark 11:24. *Therefore I say unto you, What things soever ye desire, when ye pray, believe that ye receive them, and ye shall have them* (*Ibid*).

Your end is your beginning.

Your end is where your relief, and your satisfaction, and your joy exists.

Your end is to believe that you have already received, so that you may receive.

Your end is achieved through your assumptive belief; this is the faith that will make you whole.

You can do it.

You must do it.

Your prayer must be answered.

This is *the way*.

If we believe that He hears us in all that we ask of Him, then we know that we have obtained the requests made of Him (1 John 5:15). We *have* obtained the requests.

Assume that you have obtained.

Believe it completely and confidently.

Living in the end is to remain faithful to your desired outcome regardless of whatever may attack your faith. Thoughts of doubt, or fears, or external circumstances– remain faithful to your desired outcome and your faith in the end will make you whole.

Living in the end requires you to journey through a period of incubation of your prayer. There is, in my opinion, a verse of scripture that has been misunderstood and misapplied for centuries, as it contains a dual meaning hiding a principle that is another secret to the art of prayer. It is found in Matthew 17:20:

> *And Jesus said unto them, Because of your unbelief: for verily I say unto you, If ye have faith as a grain of mustard seed, ye shall say unto this mountain, Remove hence to yonder place; and it shall remove; and nothing shall be impossible unto you.*

If you have *faith as a grain of mustard seed.* It has been taught that this speaks to the "volume" or "size" of faith; however, there is an unknown dual meaning hidden within this text– a mustard seed takes nine days to sprout.

Nine is the sacred number in the Hebrew text used to establish the man or woman who is complete in the grace of God in the fullness of the power of God.

Nine symbolizes Divine completeness, or conveys the meaning of finality.

A mustard seed sprouts in nine days– nine days to establish you in the fullness and completeness of God's grace.

If you have faith as a grain of mustard seed– if you can remain faithful unto completeness and fullness, you shall say to your problem (mountain), "Remove hence to yonder place, and it shall remove, and NOTHING shall be impossible to you!"

Everything has an interval of time. If we know that He hears us in all that we ask of Him, then we know that we have obtained the requests made of Him, but there is an interval of time required to see the realization of our request.

There is a definite interval between our imaginal act and its fulfillment, just as there is an interval of time between the physical creative act between a man and woman and the birth of the child. A child requires nine months. A mustard seed takes nine days.

The Bible teaches us that every "vision" has its appointed hour. It will ripen and flower, as it is found in Habakkuk:

> *And the Lord answered me, and said, Write the vision, and make it plain upon tables, that he may run that readeth it. For the vision is yet for an appointed time, but at the end it shall speak, and not lie: though it tarry, wait for it;*

because it will surely come, it will not tarry.
Behold, his soul which is lifted up is not upright
in him: but the just shall live by his faith (Hab.
2:2-4)."

Take instruction and comfort when your prayer
seems delayed. He said, *"though it tarry"*. When your
prayers appear to be slow in coming, or "tarrying", just
wait for it. Why? Because it will surely come, and
even though it *seems late*, it will not tarry. It is sure
and it will not be late– it's simply the interval of time
required to incubate your desire. Therefore, live in the
end and be patient in the knowledge that it is finished.

I have, since April of 2023, seen this time and
time again. There is an interval of time required. I can
also attest to the fact that I have seen my prayers
answered in an hour, and others have taken weeks.

Hold fast to your assumptive belief and it will
materialize and harden into a fact. *As a man thinketh*
in his heart, so is he.

When you approach God's throne humbly in
prayer and make your petitions known, and when you
receive your requests as though you already have them
through your imaginal act of creating the ending scene

of having your desire, and feeling that relief and satisfaction and rejoicing over having received your petitions, nothing– no man and nothing– *no thing* can stop it!

You will find as you remain faithful to the outcome the entire world will bend and flex toward your resultant outcome. The transformative unfolding of events in the direction of your answered prayer will shock and astonish you.

This is all due to the fact that Jesus Christ is within you, for He is the Word, and the Word is with God, and the Word is God, and all things are made by Him, and without Him was not anything made that was made, for He is in the world through you, and the world was made by Him, and the world knows Him not.

This Word was made flesh and lives within you. He comes within you and by Him all things are possible to you.

This is the good news.

This is *the way*.

So, live in the end, and the end will harden into fact. And when the fears and doubts and circumstances strike fear into your heart, don't be confirmed to it, but be transformed by the constant and daily renewing of your mind– the mind of Jesus Christ.

Apply these principles and techniques and you will transform your world.

Tonight, examine yourself to see whether you are holding to the faith. Test yourself, for do you not know that Jesus Christ is within you?

For he saith, I have heard thee in a time accepted, and in the day of salvation have I succored thee: behold, now is the accepted time; behold, now is the day of salvation (2 Cor. 6:2).

Live in the end, for your end is your beginning.

<u>24</u>

Modern "Manifestation" Movement

"You've got to share this, Michael," she said with conviction.

"It's too radical," I admitted.

"It's not radical– it's unknown, and it's Jesus' teachings. You're proving it over and over in our lives," she pressed.

I had been with her since 1983, and I've never seen her misjudge anything. Yes, I know, it sounds like an extreme exaggeration, but I assure you it's not.

Jonetta has an uncanny ability to observe, to weigh, to consider, and to dispense an uncommon wisdom. I've never seen her wisdom and advice fail– in almost 40 years of being with her, I've not seen her wrong one single time. Not. One. Single. Time.

"I don't know," I admitted. "It's absolutely true, but members of the church might think it's some kind of weird, 'New Age' thing."

"Listen," she reasoned, "think about all that's happened. Think about the fact that God has given you the gift of knowing the mystery that Jesus is within. Our prayers are being answer as never before– don't you want others to know and experience this kind of practical faith?"

"Of course I do," I responded. "But–"

"But what?"

"But, there's a lot of new age '*woo-woo*' on social media right now, and look at all of the 'manifestation' stuff being peddled."

"Good point," she admitted as she contemplated my response. "God's word, Michael."

"What do you mean?"

"The modern Manifestation Movement– what is it based on?" she asked.

I thought about it… "The principals they're using comes from Jesus Christ– they come from the Bible, but there's a segment of the movement that don't want Christ or the Bible. They want the power and benefits, but they don't want the Bible."

"Michael," she said as I could see that she had come to the point, "Jesus is the way, the truth, and the life. The people in the manifestation movement– those who reject Jesus and His Word are the robbers, aren't they?"

"Wait, what?"

"Honey, get your Bible," she said with a smile. John 10:1-2 says:

Verily, verily, I say unto you, He that entereth not by the door into the sheepfold, but climbeth

There is a movement today that is, what I call, the modern Manifestation Movement (MM). The MM uses the principles found within Mark 11:24 to "manifest" reality.

Promoters in MM sell subscribers on the idea of riches and fame and health and wealth by following their particular "affirmations, scripting, and money-mindset" ideas.

There seems to be a large segment of the MM that rejects the Bible and Jesus Christ; however, they freely admit that all of manifestation originates from and rests upon the principles found in the Bible.

They seem to want the pearl of great price without having to sell all that they own.

They seem to want the riches of all blessings in Christ Jesus without having to surrender their lives to Christ by obeying the gospel.

To take what is not yours is to be a thief– a robber. If a man attempts to gain access to the blessings and power of Christ by entering in by a doorway that is not Christ, is he not climbing up in some other way? Is he not the same as a thief and a robber?

I don't want to misapply the scriptures, and I do not want to disparage the thousands– maybe millions, who are involved in the MM. As a matter of fact, I've seen many involved in the MM on social media who are, without a doubt, good people. They seem to be good hearted, loving, sincere, genuine, honest people who are seeking the blessings of God.

And please forgive any statement that implied that everyone in the MM rejects the Lord and His Word– that isn't my intention and that is not what I am saying or implying.

Here's the point: I assert that there is no salvation in any other, for there is none other name under heaven given among men whereby we must be saved (Acts 4:12), and that name is Jesus Christ.

I, furthermore, assert that only in Jesus Christ are all spiritual blessings received and enjoyed (Eph. 1:3).

I assert that one must obey the gospel (Acts 2:38), and in doing so the Lord adds that one to His body, the church (Acts 2:47; Col. 1:18). Obedience to the gospel puts that one into Jesus Christ (Romans 6:3-6) and makes that one a child of God by faith in Jesus, which makes that one Abraham's seed and an heir– a true heir according to the promise (Gal. 3:26-29).

I believe that, according to my understanding, if someone attempts to gain access as an heir without having obeyed the gospel, he may be attempting to climb up in some other way, and such an act would make that one as a thief and a robber.

The blessings that come by learning Christ's words and principles toward the discipline and practice required to achieve a state whereby our every prayer is answered in the affirmative is buried and protected within– in Jesus Christ, as a pearl is hidden within an oyster, and protected by the outer shell and inner muscle.

Our God, in His great wisdom, foresaw that the power and wisdom of Christ could and would be misused and abused; therefore, we find that entrance into His kingdom is achieved only by the breaking and reforming of the character of mankind by the Potter.

Our hearts– our character of mind, is as clay, and must be molded by the Hand of the Potter. It must be kneaded and reshaped into a character of humility, and meekness (tamed power), and righteousness (right-thinking), and purity (a desire to avoid what is evil), and holiness (a desire to emulate the attributes of Jesus Christ) to enter into His kingdom that is within (John 17:21).

We're not deceived. We know that *neither fornicators, nor idolaters, nor adulterers, nor effeminate, nor abusers of themselves with mankind, nor thieves, nor covetous, nor drunkards, nor revilers, nor extortioners, shall inherit the kingdom of God* (1 Cor. 6:9-11).

The great stories of our time depict these principles time and time again.

I'm not a comic-book fan, but the story of Thor and the Hammer is well known. "Whoever holds this hammer gets the power of Thor", but to hold the hammer is set upon the non-negotiable rule that one must be worthy.

To obtain and operate the power of the One within us (Eph. 3:20), we must find the pearl of great price; we must then examine the requirements of "buying" the pearl– we must sell all. It is only when we "sell all", or when we willfully discard all other gods and powers and superstitions and false beliefs and false religions that we are able to buy the pearl; purchase of the pearl is made through obedience to the gospel– it is a surrender of self to Jesus Christ, and a daily mindful practice to pick up the cross and follow Him in the way.

But why would those in the MM movement choose to surrender their lives to Jesus Christ if they are, by a back-door access to the pearl, enjoying the fruits of answered prayer?

Because their lives have an expiration date– a shelf life. All men will die. Jesus said, *"For what shall it profit a man, if he shall gain the whole world, and lose his own soul?"*

What good is it to gain riches and wealth and fame if one's soul is lost at death? Why wouldn't any right-thinking person not want to enjoy *both* the abundant life offered here, *and* the eternal life He promises in the hereafter?

It, therefore, cannot be said with any legitimacy that this book and the ideas herein, originate from the modern day Manifestation Movement, just as it cannot be said that those seen taking communion are "Catholic".

In example, the Lord's Supper originated during the first century with Jesus and His disciples. This was the origin. However, the practice would (some three centuries) be taken later by the Universals (Catholics) who would rename the practice as "The Eucharist" and claim that the bread and grape juice would "transubstantiate" into the literal "flesh and blood" of Jesus.

This book is an attempt to go beyond all modern ideas– back to the original first century teaching. Let's go back beyond all of the teachings of men. Let's go back to the first century. Let's return to Jesus and His way.

We, as Christians, find our rule of faith and practice to exist not in men's rulebooks and creeds, but only in the pages of the Bible.

Am I now a Judas for revealing these secrets to you? Am I now your enemy for telling you the truth?

Jonetta was right again.

Regardless of what you may think, you need this information. You need to be reintroduced to the fact that Jesus Christ is within you.

You need to be reawakened to the good news– that Jesus came to bring you life, and life more

abundantly. You need to hear the radical idea that
your every prayer can be answered through the truths
buried deep within the text– these hidden secrets of the
art of prayer.

25
Using the Power
for Evil

It must be stated and understood that this Power that worketh within us can be used in evil and destructive ways.

The Jewish Shema is one of the most famous prayers in the Old Testament. It was a daily prayer for the Israelites, and it is still recited today.

The Shema is Deuteronomy 6:4, "*Hear, O Israel: The Lord our God is one Lord* (Deut. 6:4)." Jesus, in answering a Jewish Scribe quoted the Shema in Mark 12:29. Paul extrapolated this compound unity in Ephesians 4. John wrote, "*For there are three that bear record in heaven, the Father, the Word, and the Holy Ghost: and these three are one* (1 Jo. 5:7)."

There is but one power. "*A man can receive nothing, except it be given him from heaven* (John 3:27)."

Can a man use this one power in evil and destructive ways?

God said, "*See now that I, even I, am he, and there is no god with me: I kill, and I make alive; I wound, and I heal: neither is there any that can deliver out of my hand* (Deut. 32:39)."

God is One, and He is the Power. He kills and makes alive, He wounds, and He heals– there is no god beside Him, and none can deliver from His hand.

It was God who permitted Satan to touch Job's household (Job 1:12) via His allowance of power to Satan in His words, "*And the Lord said unto Satan, Behold, all that he hath is in thy power; only upon himself put not forth thine hand (Ibid)*.

This One God– the Creator and Father, holds per conveys His power; there is no other power or god.

Jesus Christ within us is that Power that works within us (Eph. 3:20). We, as the operant power, meaning that we wield His power via our imaginative faculties, can imagine evil. We can, within prayer, immerse (baptize) ourselves into that evil imaginative creation and be surrounded in it to the point that we feel the feeling. And if one lives within that feeling, it will manifest.

All of Hollywood, and secret societies, and witchcraft, and sorcery, and the like, are perverted attempts to use the one true power of God.

This is why it is so dangerous to dabble and play with such things.

Jesus, our Potter, is telling you that to imagine in your heart is to have done the act. Why? Because your imaginal act, whether righteous, or whether an act of adultery, is the power of creation, and is equivalent to bringing the unseen into the seen. *"Even God, who quickeneth the dead, and calleth those things which be not as though they were (Rom. 4:17)."*

You already know at your core that this is true. Jesus said, *"Ye have heard that it was said by them of old time, Thou shalt not commit adultery: But I say unto you, That whosoever looketh on a woman to lust after her hath committed adultery with her already in his heart (Matt. 5:27-28)."*

When you create an imaginal act within your mind, you are using the one power of the Potter, and every thought is a seed that has within itself the power to spring forth and bear fruit– and if it be an evil seed, the harvest will be a fruit of pain, sadness, and destruction.

I cannot tell anyone what to do– I can only acquaint you with the truth, but remember God's words, *"I call heaven and earth to record this day against you, that I have set before you life and death, blessing and cursing: therefore, choose life, that both thou and thy seed may live (Deut. 30:19)."*

I encourage you in love– please choose life, and do good unto all men. Do everything from the restraint of love.

26

Fear is the Enemy

Fear.

It is the enemy of the mind.

Everything you desire is on the other side of fear.

Daniel prayed to the Lord for the preservation of life; his life was on the other side of the lions – the other side of fear.

You want life, and life more abundantly. *That* life is on the other side of fear.

Your life is comprised of memories of the past, the reality of today, and your thoughts of tomorrow. All exists within your mind.

History– your past, exists only within your mind. The future is unknown; therefore, it can exist only within your mind.

The most powerful material thing in this world is your mind. There is no computer or technology that comes close to the power which is your mind.

Your mind– the mind of Christ, fashions and forms. As you think in your mind, so are you (Prov. 23:7).

You must attend to your mind.

As you cannot prevent a bird from landing on your head, you *can* prevent him from building a nest.

I read a story of a man with stage four terminal cancer who, after getting into a car wreck and waking with amnesia, was diagnosed a few months later as "cancer free". The doctors called it a miracle.

The man forgot he had cancer. He went to no doctors, and took no treatments. All of his attention was removed from the idea entirely. His cancer disappeared. The power of the mind.

What we give attention to grows. What we remove our attention from shrinks. Our attention acts as sunlight and water to nourish and grow the seeds in our garden.

"Fear is our survival response," explains Zachary Sikora, PsyD, a Clinical Psychologist at Northwestern Medicine. While some people, like roller-coaster enthusiasts and horror movie fans, seek out fear for the thrill, others tend to avoid it. But have you ever wondered why?

Fear is Physical. Although fear begins in the mind, it triggers a powerful physical reaction in the body. When you encounter something frightening, the amygdala, a small organ located in the brain's center, springs into action. It alerts the nervous system, initiating the body's fear response. This leads to the release of stress hormones such as cortisol and adrenaline. Your blood pressure and heart rate spike, and your breathing becomes rapid. Even your blood flow changes, diverting away from your heart and towards your limbs, readying you to either fight or flee. This is your body's preparation for the fight-or-flight response (Northwester Medicine, Dr. Zachary Sikora, PsyD., *5 Things You Never Knew About Fear*, October 2020; nm.org).

Why did Paul tell us to think on things that are noble and right and pure and lovely and admirable, and things that are excellent and praiseworthy? Because God is, through Paul, telling you to tend to your garden. He is telling you to plant good seeds and to give them water and light. We are, in this way, to have the mind of Christ.

In his book *Unlimited Power: The New Science Of Personal Achievement*, acclaimed speaker, bestselling author, and life coach Anthony Robbins shares the remarkable story of a psychiatric patient with dissociative identity disorder. This woman exhibited multiple distinct personalities, each with its own unique characteristics. What was particularly astounding was how her body physically adapted to the different needs and conditions of each personality. One of her personalities had diabetes, while another did not. When the diabetic personality was in control, her blood sugar levels would rise, and she would display all the symptoms of diabetes. However, as soon as she transitioned to a different personality, her blood sugar levels normalized, and all signs of diabetes disappeared. It was as if two different individuals inhabited the same body, with each mind influencing the body's biological functions accordingly.

This case, among others, highlights the profound influence the mind can have over the body. It suggests that through the power of the mind, individuals can seemingly alter their physical states and health conditions, demonstrating an extraordinary connection between mental and physical well-being.

In another story, Stamatis Moraitis, a Greek war veteran, had settled in the United States when his life took an unexpected turn. He was diagnosed with terminal lung cancer, with doctors giving him only nine months to live. They proposed aggressive treatments to slow the disease's progression, but these would not ultimately save his life and came with a high financial and physical cost.

Choosing a different path, Stamatis decided to forgo the treatment and moved back to his native Ikaria, a Greek island, with his wife. He wished to spend his remaining days there and be buried among his ancestors. They settled into a small house with his elderly parents, and Stamatis embraced each day as if it were his last. He spent time in church, reconnected with old friends, tended to his garden, enjoyed the island's sunshine, and cherished his wife.

Contrary to the grim prognosis, Stamatis's health began to improve. He grew stronger and more vibrant with each passing day. Years later, curious about his miraculous recovery, he returned to the United States to consult his doctors, only to find that they had all passed away. Stamatis continued to thrive, living to the remarkable age of 102.

Anita Moorjani had a profound near-death experience that she recounts in her book *Dying To Be Me*. After a lengthy battle with lymphoma, her condition deteriorated to Stage 4, and she felt she was nearing the end of her life. During this time, she experienced the classic "white light" phenomenon often associated with near-death experiences. In this state, she was given a choice: to either leave her tumor-ridden body or return to life and share her story with others.

Despite her reluctance to return due to the immense pain and suffering, a mysterious voice assured her that she could be healed. Trusting in this promise, Anita chose to live.

Remarkably, her recovery was swift and complete; within weeks, her cancer had vanished. Medical teams were astounded by her spontaneous remission, thoroughly documenting her case. Now, Anita shares her incredible story, spreading the message that death is not something to fear (Three stories adapted from 4 Inspiring Stories That May Prove That Mind is Over Matter, Ajit Ludher, June 15, 2019. Public Blog Post, ludher.net).

To entertain fear is to pray.

Fear is an unpleasant emotion caused by the belief that someone or something is dangerous, likely to cause pain, or a threat. When we entertain the thoughts of fear, we are "imagining" the worst. Imagining the worst is our mind creating pictures of unwanted, dreadful outcomes.

A *feeling is created by the imagining* of these pictures – when you marry your thoughts with emotions, you are creating the outcome.

You are, thereby, praying.

As a man thinketh in his heart, so is he (Prov. 23:7). *Pray without ceasing* – you are always praying, and you are never ceasing from praying, because you are always talking and "picturing" in your mind.

The mind is referred to by the Lord as "the chamber of imagery". Ezekiel 8:12 says:

Then said he unto me, Son of man, hast thou seen what the ancients of the house of Israel do in the dark, every man in the chambers of his imagery? For they say, the Lord seeth us not; the Lord hath forsaken the earth.

It is within this chamber of imagery – our imagination, that we create images and pictures done in the dark of our minds, and the Lord sees and acts upon what we do in the dark.

"I can't turn it off!" you exclaim.

Yes, you're right– you can't turn it off.

You must, instead, change your inner talk.

To think and to speak within is to imagine, and to imagine is to sow; therefore, you are forever sowing seed in the soil of your garden.

When you give your mind over to Jesus Christ and make your mind "His mind," you operate from the mind of Christ (1 Cor. 2:16). This mind of Christ creates through imagining on the best for self and others. You reject and neutralize all unloving and unkind thoughts, thereby removing bad seeds and weeds from your garden. You begin to sow only the kind and loving seeds, and your creative acts will rise to meet you in the future.

This is tending to your garden. You must, instead, learn to stop the negative and fearful thoughts by recognizing your thoughts for what they are, then rejecting the unwanted thoughts, and then replacing the unwanted thoughts by the thought that you desire.

This is a discipline that is learned through constant effort over a period of time. And it is through this practice that you learn to cease from being confirmed by this world, and to be transformed by the renewing of your mind.

This discipline is minute-by-minute, hour-by-hour, day-by-day, and it never stops. It requires practice, and patience, and forgiveness. It requires a commitment to always be on guard over your garden.

Fear is the great enemy. Fear will enter in quickly and deposit the thought into your garden. If not caught early, an emotion will be produced, and the seed will take root.

Dear reader, fear not.

"Fear thou not; for I am with thee: be not dismayed; for I am thy God: I will strengthen thee; yea, I will help thee; yea, I will uphold thee with the right hand of my righteousness (Isa. 41:10)."

"Fear not, little flock; for it is your Father's good pleasure to give you the kingdom (Luke 12:32)."

Everything you desire is on the other side of fear.

I am steadfastly convinced in my conviction that prayer, when the art is properly understood and the elements employed as revealed in this story and within Scripture, will give to every man the promise of a more abundant life that was promised by our Lord. The concepts in this story not new – we've just missed them.

–Author

27
Test Him and See

We have experienced numerous results that are nothing short of miraculous. Most are too personal to share with you in this public venue, because they have been answers to personal issues, but here's a few results that I *can* share publicly...

Jonetta broke her wrist in February of this year. She had surgery, then followed up with a specialist at his office several times from February to June.

During a May appointment, Jonetta and I were waiting in one of the specialist's exam rooms. The specialist's office manager, "Dorothy", was having a conversation with another staff member. They were both standing just outside of our exam room.

Dorothy looked to be in her mid-sixties. We'd found out through a few casual conversations with her that she had worked for the doctor since 2001, starting as a medical transcriptionist and working her way up to her current role as Office Manager. Dorothy was kind and personable. She told us that she'd never had any children and lived alone.

"I'll have to work till I'm 80," we heard Dorothy say to her coworker. "I've just never made enough for a retirement. I can't even afford to eat—groceries are just out of control!"

"We should have married rich men, Dorothy!" laughed her coworker in response.

"Oh, I wish I'd married anyone!" laughed Dorothy. The women finished their conversation and went on about their business.

"Let's pray for her," Jonetta whispered as she leaned in close to me.

I smiled. "For what?"

"We know the law. Let's imagine the best for her," said Jonetta into my ear.

"Right now?" I asked.

"Yeah, right now," she replied.

We closed our eyes in the quiet of the specialist's exam room. She squeezed my hand to indicate she had finished her prayer. The specialist entered our room shortly after.

About three weeks later we entered the lobby of the specialist's office for follow-up x-rays. Jonetta's arm had healed, for the most part, and the doctor wanted one final look.

The office was decorated with balloons and streamers. There was a cake on the reception counter. Someone's birthday.

A nurse took Jonetta to the x-ray machine while another escorted me to an exam room. I took a seat. Dorothy entered the room with a file under her arm and a large smile on her face.

"Hi Mr. Shank, it's nice to see you again! Your wife is doing so well with that arm," she said as she pulled a form out of the yellow folder.

"She's done great," I admitted enthusiastically, "and who's having the birthday party?"

Dorothy spun around and said, "It my retirement party!" She looked like a kid at Christmas.

"You're retiring?" I was shocked. Dorothy walked over to me as if she was getting ready to tell a secret.

"My aunt died a couple of weeks ago," said Dorothy.

"I'm sorry," I offered.

"No, no, it's perfectly fine. I didn't know her that well. She lived in Sacramento," Dorothy explained. Then her smile returned... "She left me an inheritance, so I've decided to retire."

"I'm so happy for you, Dorothy," I responded with genuine sincerity.

"Hi, Dorothy," said Jonetta as she entered the exam room after being x-rayed.

"Honey, Dorothy is retiring!" I exclaimed.

Jonetta looked at me, then Dorothy, then back to me. I could see it on her face.

"Well, aren't you going to congratulate her?" I asked with a smile.

"Oh, yes, I'm sorry, Dorothy, congratulations!" Jonetta hugged Dorothy in the excitement of it all.

"Thank you, Mrs. Shank. It's changed my life overnight!" Dorothy said as Jonetta released her from their hug.

"It appears so, " Jonetta said emphatically.

"Her kids hate me now, though," said Dorothy as she went back to her files on the exam room counter.

"Her kids?"

"Yeah, Aunt Emma has three daughters," Dorothy responded. "Emma's sister told me that something happened a few weeks ago between Emma and her girls– some family conflict. I don't know what it was, but Aunt Emma changed her will *two days* before she died."

"You're kidding!" Jonetta's shock was palpable, and I could feel a lump forming in my throat as Dorothy detailed what had happened.

"I know, I can't believe it either! Aunt Dorothy named me and her nephew as the sole inheritors of her estate," Dorothy beamed. "I'm still in a state of shock!"

I wasn't looking in a mirror, but my mouth had to be hanging open at that moment. Jonetta looked as though she'd seen a ghost. She was pale. We signed some forms and Dorothy bounced out of the room. She was on cloud nine.

"Michael!" Jonetta blurted as she grabbed my arm.

"I know, I know– what did you pray that day?" Jonetta and I hadn't talked about our prayer for Dorothy that we'd said in the exam room three weeks before.

"I don't remember exactly, but I imagined her being retired, and having money, and being financially comfortable," she responded. I could see her mentally retracing what she'd done in her mind. "Then I just...

well, I just said in my mind that it was done. Jesus had
done it! Didn't know how, He just done it!"

"Have you thought about it since," I asked.

"No, have you?" Jonetta asked.

"Hadn't given it a second thought," I admitted.

We started to laugh. It was that uncontrollable
laughter you get when you're filled with joy. Jonetta
hugged me as we laughed harder. Dorothy had no idea
that we'd overheard her conversation during our
previous visit, and she had no idea we'd prayed for her.

"Wait a minute, what did you pray?" Jonetta
asked as she leaned back out of my arms to look at my
eyes.

"I imagined I could hear her saying to her staff
that she was retiring, and I imagined I could hear the
others congratulating her," I said.

"You imagined this party?" Jonetta asked with
excitement.

"No, no, I didn't imagine this party, but I did
imagine her coworkers being happy for her."

We had prayed for Dorothy *in His name*. We
imagined in our heart a scene that implied the answer
to our prayer. We immersed ourself into the feeling of
our wish fulfilled. We felt, within our prayer,

Dorothy's joy and happiness in our imaginal scene. We "*believe*[d] *that ye receive them* (Mark 11:24)," as Christ taught. Then, we dropped it. We knew that it was done, and we didn't give it a second thought.

Assumptive belief. Live in the wish fulfilled and your assumption will harden into fact.

It would *not have just happened anyway*, as our carnal mind will try to "reason and justify" after the fact.

You are the operant power.

This means that you hold and operate the keys of the gate to the kingdom within.

You have heard that you must believe in the Word. Will you accept His offer?

What is the offer?

The answer is found in the question, what is your problem?

Sickness, depression, discouragement, finances, a job loss, broken relationships, addiction, directionless… what is your problem?

Within every problem is contained the solution therein.

Salvation to the blind mind is sight; salvation to the poor man is money; salvation to the starving man is food; salvation to the deaf is hearing; salvation to the weak is strength. What is your problem?

You see the solution.

Can you believe that all things are possible to God? Can you believe that He is within?

Accept His free gift, and go and show thyself.

If you can believe with all of your heart that Jesus Christ is the Son of God, and that God raised Him from the dead, and if you can see the solution to your problem and believe that you have already received the solution to your problem so that you will have it, then go into your closet in secret, and close the door behind you.

Enter His court with thanksgiving, and surround yourself in His answer– envelope yourself in the feeling of your wish fulfilled. Feel that feeling of how it would feel to receive your desire. Do not move or rise until that feeling fills your mind and body and soul. Rejoice with the gratitude that comes with that feeling of your wish fulfilled, and give to Him all credit, all honor, and all glory.

Rise and go forth with the confidence in knowing that you have your petition asked of Him. Decide that from that moment forth you will live in the end– you will live as if you have already received your answer.

Laugh in the face of the external circumstances which seek to instill fear, uncertainty and doubt. Experience that peace that surpasses all human understanding. Give no thought to things which oppose your answer, and tend to your garden with care and patience. To be patient, as the faith of a mustard seed. Await the incubation interval required for the Lord to bring about your answer.

Walk through the bridge of incidents that He has constructed in the knowledge that He is working all things together for your good– to the good of those who love Him and keep His commandments.

Put off the former conversation (behavior = mental thoughts in times before your answer and those actions taken in failure), and live as a new creature in Christ. Think on things that are true and honest and just and pure and lovely and of good report. Don't take your hands from the plow, and don't look back at the destruction of the city, lest you unfit yourself for the kingdom and be preserved in that state.

Be faithful unto death so that you may receive a crown of abundant life– the answer to your prayer, the

solution to your problem. The reception of that great
need in your life.

And when it appears, and you realize that the
Lord has, indeed, answered your prayers, you will
rejoice as you did within your prayer. All will rejoice.

Test it and see, my friend. You cannot
disprove it. Examine yourself at all times to see
whether you are holding to the faith– for do you not
know that Jesus Christ is in you– unless of course you
fail to meet the test.

Meet the test.

*Examine yourselves, whether ye be in the faith;
prove your own selves. Know ye not your own
selves, how that Jesus Christ is in you, except
ye be reprobates?* 2 Corinthians 13:5-7

Test Him, trust Him, and you will see for
yourself, for you cannot disprove it.

I could fill these pages with dozens of
testimonials that reveal how the Lord has answered my
prayers in the most miraculous ways over these past
few months, but time and space won't permit. Maybe,
if God wills, I will be able to share them with you in
the near future, in person.

It is my sincere hope and fervent prayer that you will test this and see for yourself, and that you will share your wonderful results with me so that I might be able to rejoice with you.

Dear reader, apply these principles in your prayers.

You have nothing to lose.

What do you have to gain? You'll come to know that mystery of Jesus Christ within you, the hope of glory!

All of this is mere heresy to you until you experience it for yourself.

There is a comfort in putting it off, because you can say, "Someday I might try it, but not today, for if I fail and find that He is not in me, all will be lost. There'll be nothing to return to."

I felt this same way... until a problem arose that required a miracle.

I was out of options. Forced to make a decision... will He answer? The choice is yours to make. Test Him and see.

Order from:
https://www.michaelshankministries.com